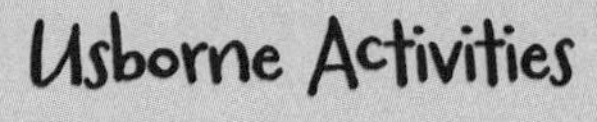

99 Math Puzzles

Written by
Sarah Khan

Designed by Marc Maynard

Illustrated by
Lizzie Barber, Non Figg and Stella Baggott

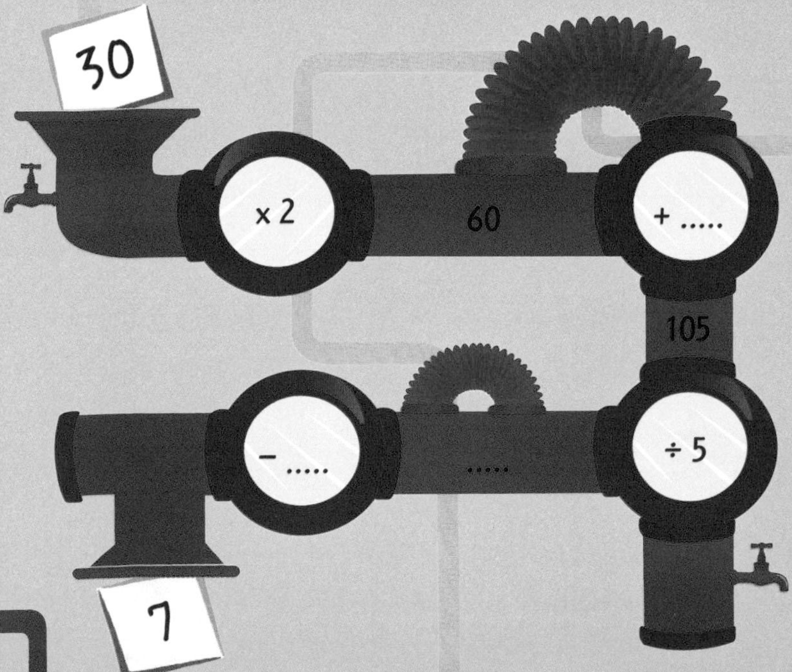

30

x 2

60

+ .....

105

÷ 5

.....

– .....

7

1

Town planning

Draw two *overlapping circles* around this town to group the buildings into three categories:

- in the top circle, buildings with **more than** three front windows
- in the bottom circle, buildings with **blue** front doors
- in the *overlap*, buildings with more than three front windows **and** a blue front door

Train travel

This train is going from Rivermouth to Forest City, stopping at Brookdale and Hilltown. At Rivermouth, 88 passengers are on the train. Some people get off at Brookdale, and 12 get on. At Hilltown, 45 people get on and 12 get off. When it reaches Forest City, there are 120 passengers on the train. How many people got off at Brookdale?

Answer: ....

ot the coordinates below on this chart, then join them
order. What shape do they make? The first number i
ch pair shows how many squares to count across fro
The second shows how many to count up or down.

4) (1, 1) (4, 1) (2, –1) (3, –4) (0, –2)

3, –4) (–2, –1) (–4, 1) (–1, 1) (0, 4)

★

Answer: ....

Dot-to-dot

Following the four times table, join the dots to see what is visiting the flowers.

Toy sales

At the start of the week, a toy store has 60 dolls, 40 balls, 55 robots and 75 teddy bears. By the end of the week, it has sold 54 dolls, 34 balls, 11 robots and 60 teddy bears.

Which toy sold the highest percentage?

Answer: ....

Honeycomb

This bee can only cross the honeycomb one cell at a time, and can only move to a cell next to the one it's in. Draw the shortest route it can take to reach its friend, only crossing the cells that contain even numbers.

Milk monitor

A farmer has five cows – April, Buttercup, Clara, Daisy and Edna. He draws a chart to show how many units of milk each cow gives in one day, but forgets to write down their names. All he can remember is that April gave one unit more than Clara, and that Edna gave the same amount as Buttercup.

How many units did each cow produce?

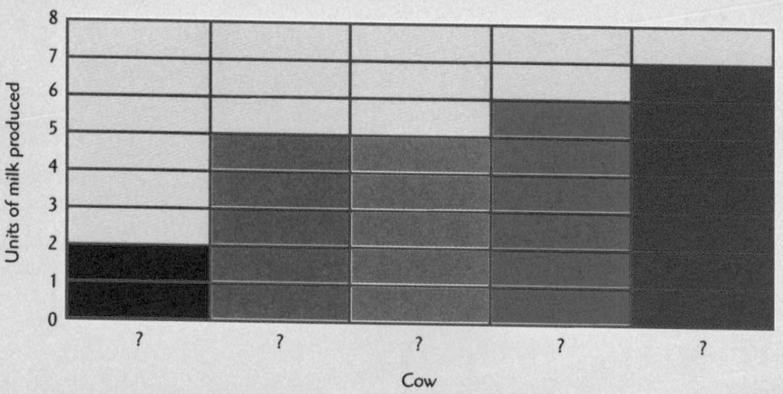

April ....

Buttercup ....

Daisy ....

Clara ....

Edna ....

Bags and cases

A group of people are waiting for a train. Altogether, they have ten pieces of luggage.

- They have two blue bags and one blue suitcase.
- They have one less green bag than blue bags.
- They have one more black suitcase than blue suitcases.
- The number of brown bags is equal to the number of green bags and the number of black suitcases added together. The rest of the bags are red.

How many items of luggage are:

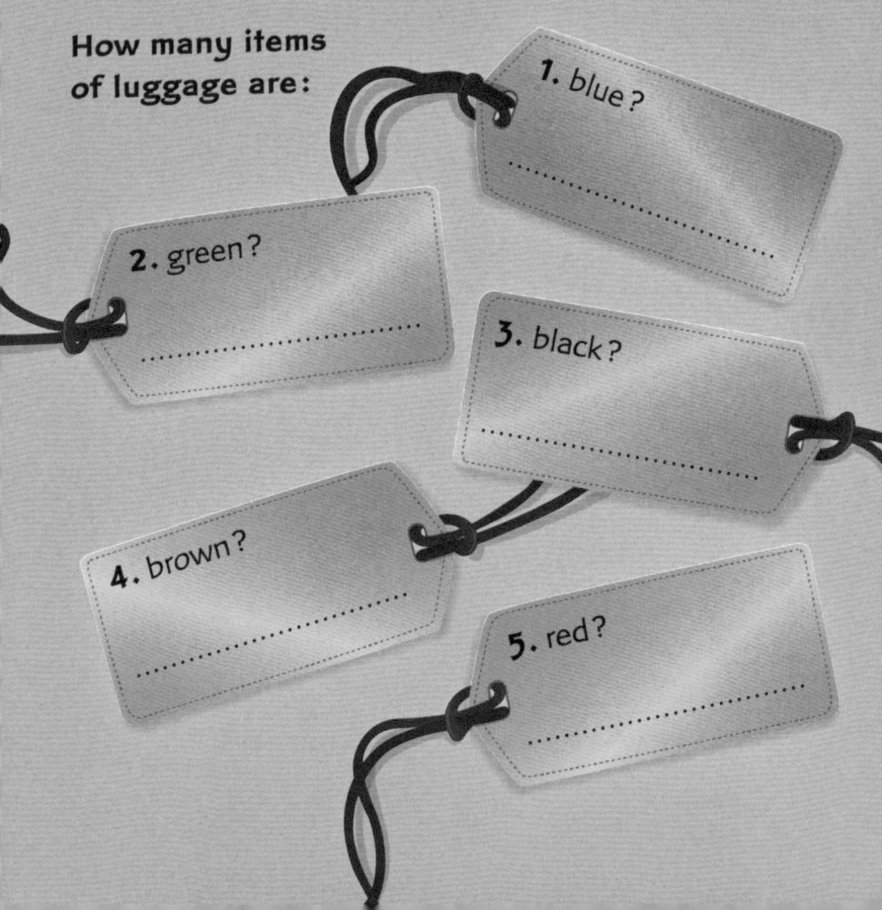

9 Bubblegum machine

There are 20 pieces of bubblegum in this bubblegum machine. Ten pieces are red, one piece is yellow and the rest are green. Draw lines to join the questions below to their correct answers. When you put a coin in the machine, what's the chance of the piece of gum that falls out being...

... red?	**Unlikely**
... yellow?	**Even chance**
... green or red?	**Impossible**
... blue?	**Likely**
...bubblegum?	**Definite**

Long flight

Jack is flying from Sydney, Australia, to New York City, USA, stopping off in Los Angeles on the way. Use the information below to calculate what the time and date will be in New York when he arrives.

- Jack's flight leaves Sydney at 2:00 p.m. on Tuesday, November 30th.
- New York is 12 hours behind Sydney, so when it's the middle of the morning in New York, it's already the middle of the evening in Sydney.
- The flight from Los Angeles to New York takes five hours.
- The flight from Sydney to Los Angeles takes 14 hours.
- Jack's stop in Los Angeles is two hours.

Answer:

....

....

Chocolate factory

This graph shows information about the production of milk chocolates and chocolate caramels in a factory. Can you use it to answer the questions below?

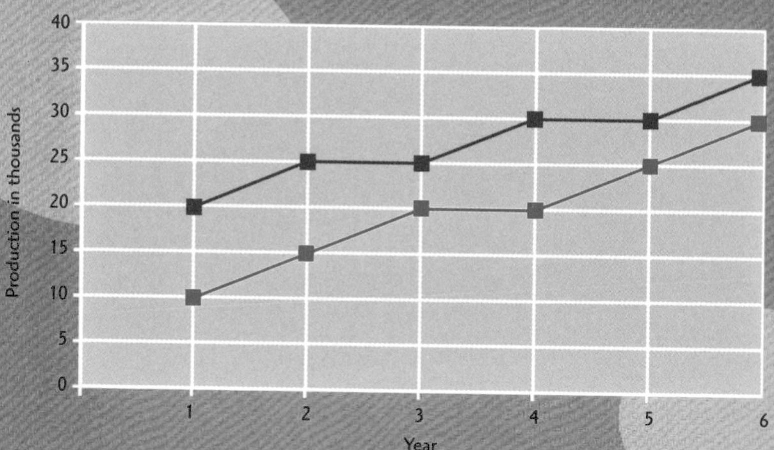

Chocolate caramel production   Milk chocolate production

1. The production of which type of chocolates increased the most between Years 1 and 6? Circle the answer.

2. The production of which type of chocolates increased the least between Years 2 and 5? Underline the answer.

3. By how much did chocolate caramel production increase between Years 4 and 6?

Answer:..

Towers and turrets

Draw a new tower on the grid, exactly the same shape, but moved six squares to the right and five squares up.

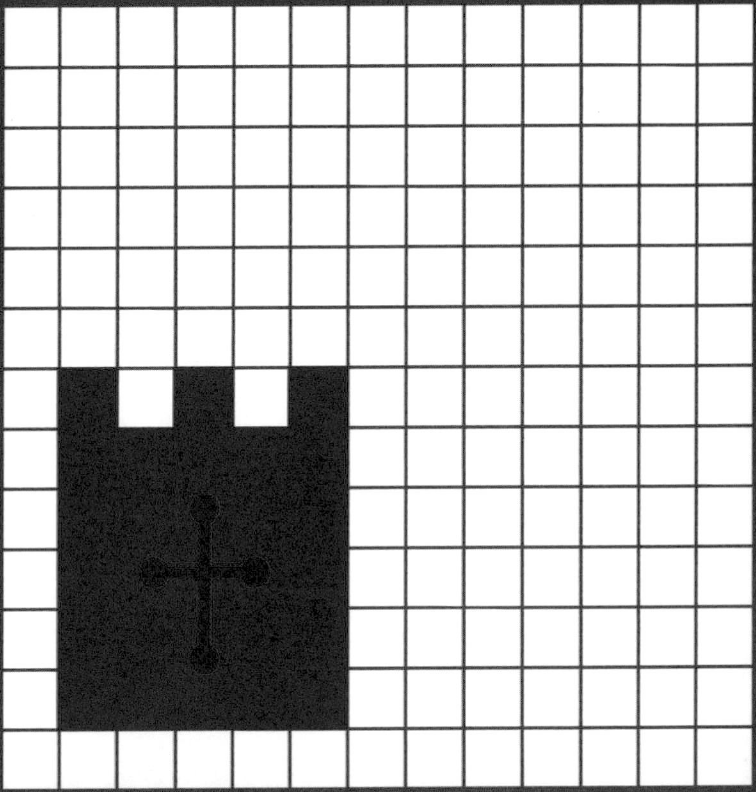

13

A game of golf

This golfer wants to walk from his tee to all four holes in order, taking the shortest route and avoiding the sand bunkers and the water. He can only walk north, south, east and west. How many steps will he have to take?

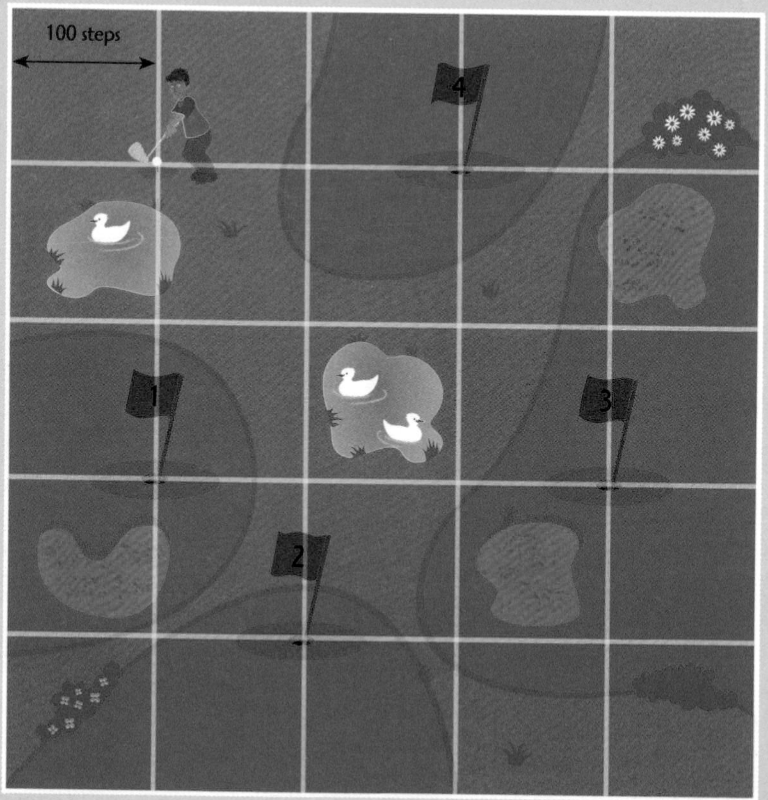

100 steps

Answer:

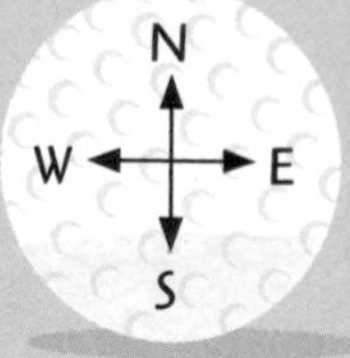

....

Missing symbols

Fill in the missing symbols to make each line true. Use < for "is less than", > for "is more than" and = for "is equal to".

a. 0.75 .... $\frac{3}{4}$

b. $\frac{1}{4}$ .... $\frac{90}{270}$

c. -87 .... -78

d. 24.564 .... 24.465

e. 20% .... $\frac{1}{5}$

f. 1, 000, 000 .... one hundred thousand

g. 846, 372 .... 846, 382

h. $\frac{5}{15}$ .... $\frac{7}{21}$

i. 394 .... three hundred and ninety four

j. six hundred and forty two 6.42

15

Pool party

The manager of Hotel Tropicana is in charge of a kids' club at the hotel, and is making a note of the children's ages and nationalities. She starts putting this information into a table but, before she can complete it, she drops her notes into the pool.

Can you help her fill in the missing numbers?

	Under 10	10 – 16	Total
American	5		8
British	7	4	
German		9	18
French	6		10
Total		20	

Market day

If you take 25 coins to market and buy everything on the shopping list at the bottom of the page, how many coins will you have left?

Shopping list

3 carrots	4 apples
1 pumpkin	1 cauliflower
5 potatoes	$\frac{1}{2}$ bag berries

Answer:

....

17

Gaming challenge

Answers:

1. Justin has 55 computer games. Three out of every 11 are strategy games, and the rest are racing games. How many racing games does he have? ....

2. Justin takes part in a gaming tournament. He wins three out of every four games he plays. If he wins 12 games, how many games does he lose? ....

3. There are 30 competitors, and one in every five of them is a girl. How many fewer girls than boys are taking part? ....

Parallel lines

Draw an X on the train track that runs parallel to the track that the train is on.

Odd one out

Do the calculations, then circle the *odd one out* in each set.

A

52 – 48

15 ÷ 5

0.25 x 12

–17 + 20

B

–4 + 11

0.5 x 15

56 ÷ 8

93 – 86

C

67 – 52

60 ÷ 5

0.75 x 20

–19 + 34

D

144 ÷ 3

111 – 63

0.2 x 220

–33 + 81

Along the line

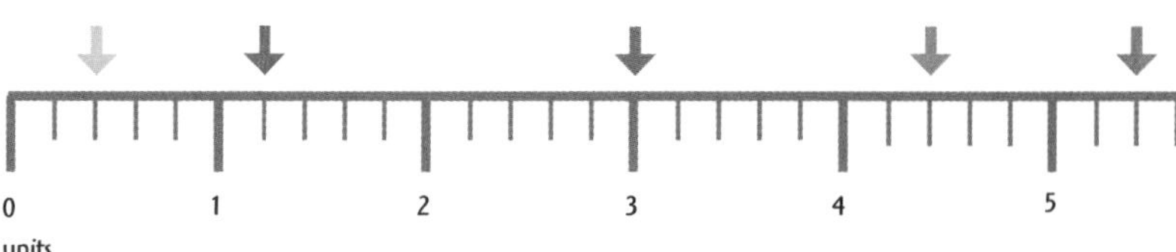

What's the distance between ...

1. ... the green arrow and the blue arrow?

....

2. ... the pink arrow and the purple arrow?

....

3. ... the blue arrow and the orange arrow?

....

4. ... the green arrow and the orange arrow?

....

21

Rabbit holes

There's only time for three rabbits to jump down each hole before the fox arrives. How many rabbits will have to run away?

Answer: ....

Counting cookies

1. Hannah bakes some cookies. She gives half of them to her friend, but then she drops half of the cookies that she has left. Now she only has six cookies. How many did she have to start with?

Answer:...

2. Hannah spends the next day baking more cookies. She eats three, then divides the rest into seven boxes. She puts one cookie in the first box, two in the second, four in the third and so on, doubling the number for each box. How many cookies did she bake?

Answer:...

+ =?

Triangle count

How many triangles are there in this pattern?

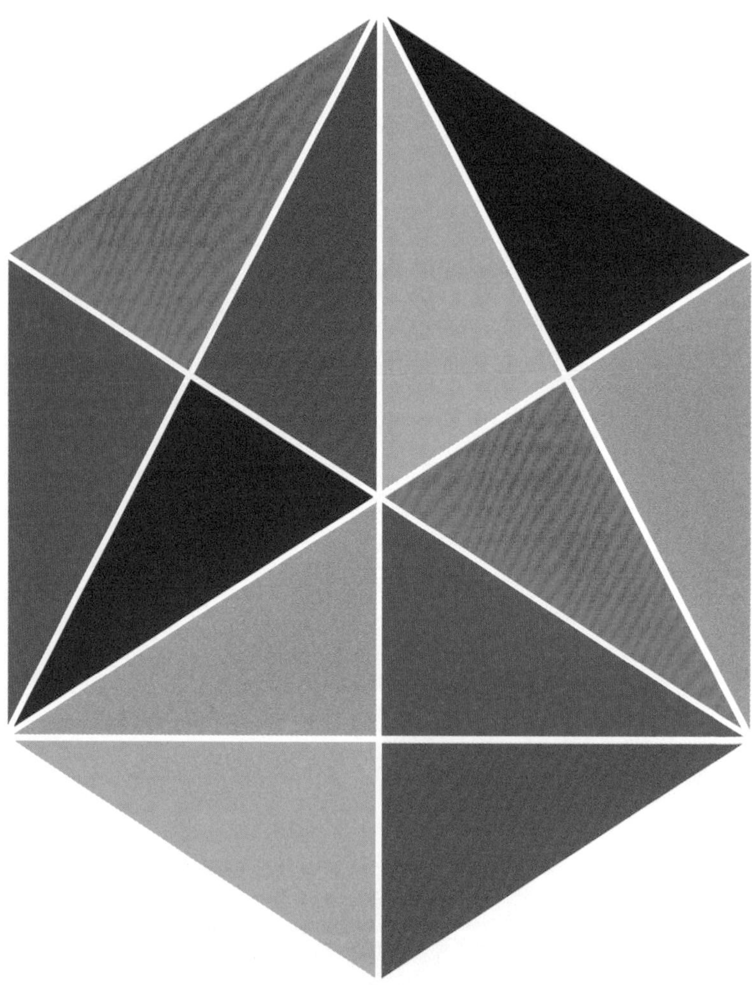

Answer: ....

Frog and flies

Every time Frodo the frog feels hungry, he moves clockwise, flicks out his tongue to catch a fly, then goes back to his original position. Write the order in which the flies will be eaten if he turns at these angles:

180°, 90°, 270°, 315°, 135°

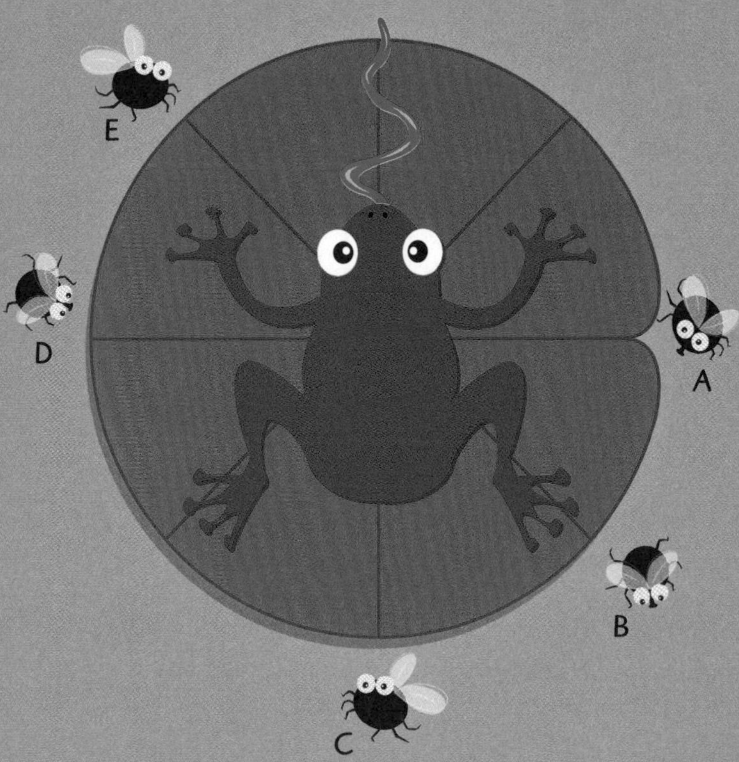

Answer: ....

Crazy rides

This graph shows information about the number of people going on different rides in Crazy Town Theme Park. Can you use it to answer the questions below?

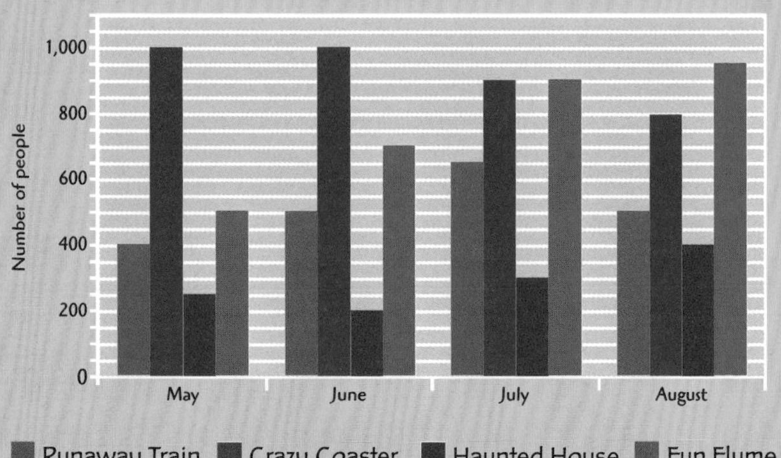

1. Circle the month that had the most visitors to the park.

2. Underline the most popular ride between May and August.

3. How many more visitors went on the Fun Flume in July than in May?

Answer:..

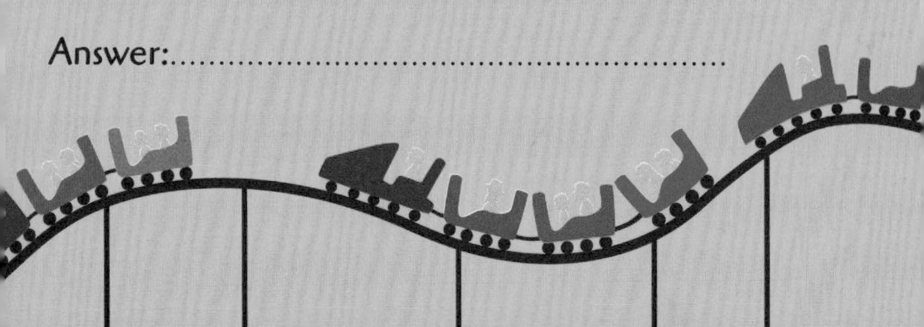

Cross-number

Use the clues to put the correct numbers into the grid.

Across →	Down ↓
2. 40,000 x 5	**1.** 6,308 + 3,601
4. twelve million, forty-three thousand and seven	**3.** three quarters, as a decimal
6. one fifth, as a decimal	**4.** one million and eleven
8. the number of months in five thousand years	**5.** the number of degrees in a full circle x 1,001
9. 47,893,748 – 6,351,454	**7.** 38,695 + 42,179

27

Total Talent

Here are the results of the text and phone votes for the latest round of a TV singing competition, "Total Talent". Look at the scores, then see if you can answer the questions below.

Votes received

Mischa	Text - 958,273	Phone - 1,107,475
Louis	Text - 964,529	Phone - 979,768
Ellie	Text - 974,702	Phone - 988,021
Rob	Text - 978,504	Phone - 1,045,371
Jordan	Text - 899,878	Phone - 998,796

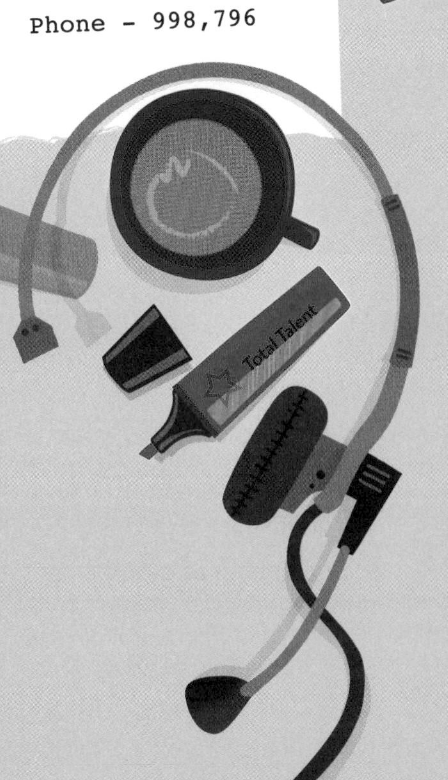

1. Can you underline the names of the three contestants with the most votes?

2. Can you draw an X by the name of the contestant who got the fewest votes?

On target

Each ring on the target below represents a score.

If you fire three arrows, and hit different rings, which three rings would you have to hit to score:

70 ....

100 ....

120 ....

(There may be more than one way to make up a score.)

Can tower

Write the missing numbers on the blank can labels. Each number is the sum of the two directly underneath it.

Safe cracker

Follow the instructions to discover the combination for the safe. Every time you turn the dial, you move a new number to the top. Start with 0 at the top of the dial.

Answers:

Turn the dial 10% clockwise.	....
Then, turn the dial 20% in the opposite direction.	....
Then, turn the dial 40% clockwise.	....
Lastly, turn the dial 60% in the opposite direction.	....

Giant rocket

Draw a new rocket on the grid, exactly the same shape, but twice as big. The first part has been done for you.

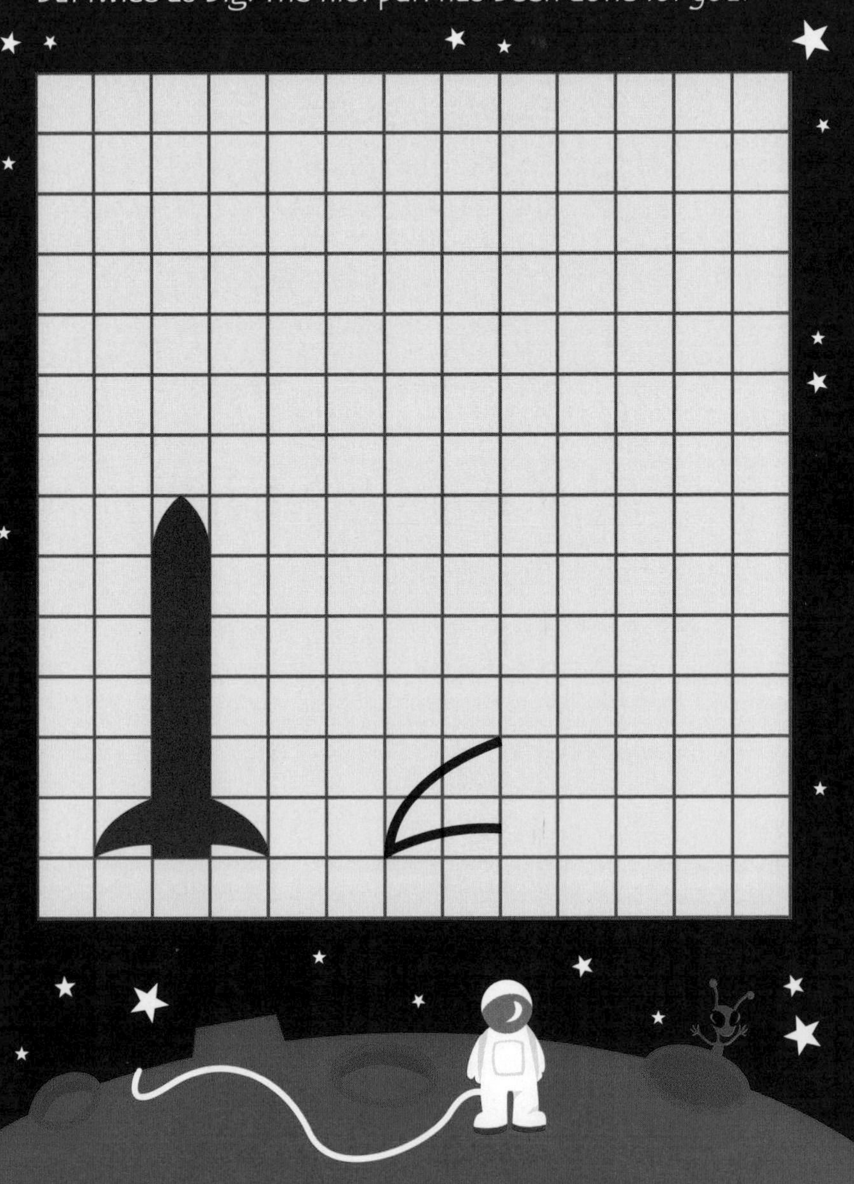

Inside numbers

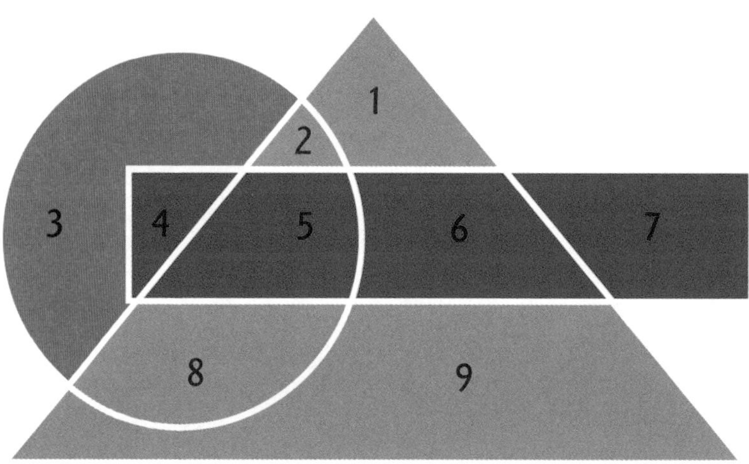

Answers:

1. Which number is inside both the circle and the rectangle, but not the triangle?	....
2. Which numbers are inside both the triangle and the circle, but not the rectangle?	....
3. Which numbers are only inside the triangle and *no other* shape?	....
4. Which number is inside all three shapes?	....

Gone fishing

Each person can only catch a fish that's equal to the number in front of them. Circle the child who won't catch anything and the fish that will get away.

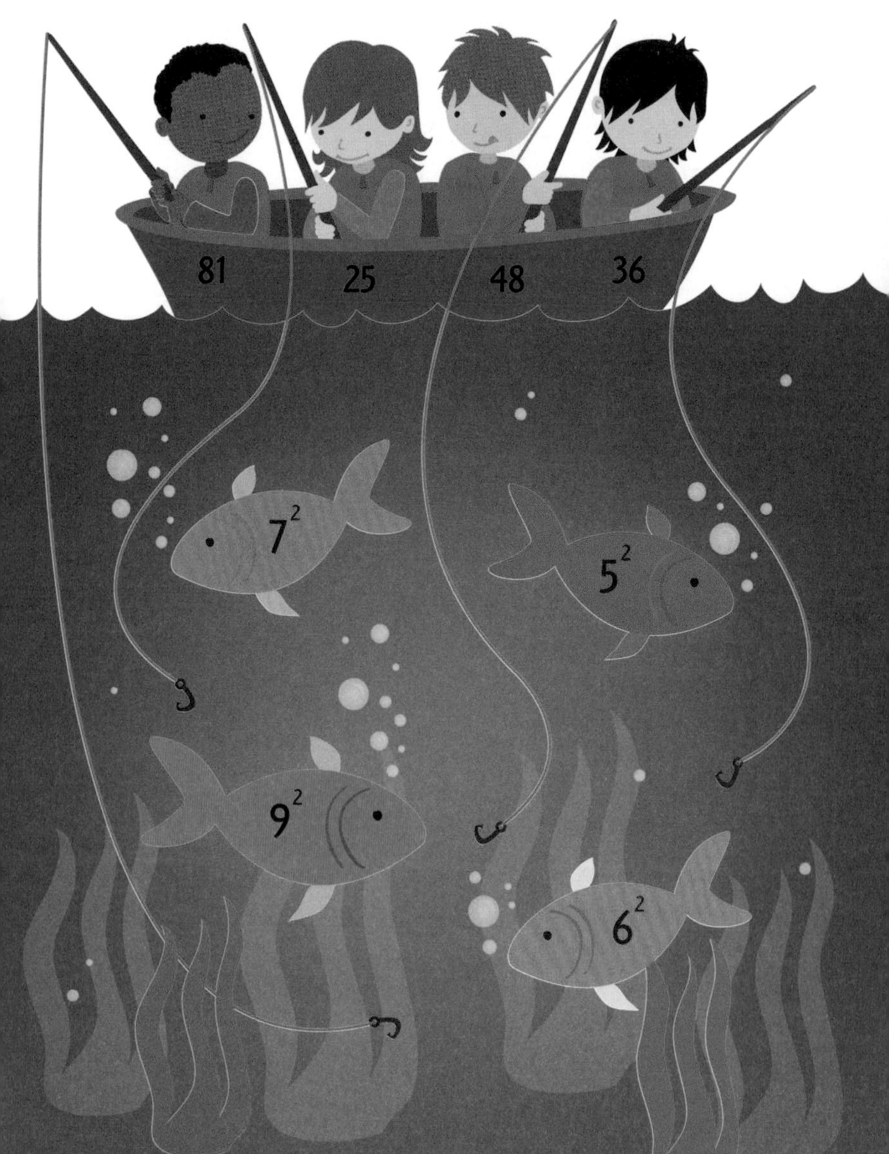

Gridlock

Tom and Katie are stuck in traffic. Tom looks out of his window and sees 2 red cars, 3 blue cars, and 5 silver cars. Katie looks out of her window and sees 6 silver cars, 3 black cars, 2 blue cars, and 1 red car.

What percentage of
Tom's cars are red? ....

What percentage of
Katie's cars are black? ....

What percentage of all the cars
both drivers can see are silver? ....

Bingo challenge

Ravi and Josh are playing Brain-bending Bingo. When a number is called out, they have to cross off the square on their card that links to that number. Look at the bingo cards below and the numbers that are called, then circle the name of the person who will complete his card first.

Ravi

45x2	22–14	99÷3
52+24	84÷7	70–11
4x16	63+21	57–36

Josh

6x14	108÷9	16+43
98–22	17+47	5x18
96÷12	73–51	18+15

Code calculator

The answer to each of the calculations below is represented by a letter. See if you can do the calculations, then match the letters to the corresponding answers at the bottom of the page to solve the riddle.

Riddle: Which side of a cow has the most hair?

Calculations:

75 x 3 = O 379 – 254 = E 512 ÷ 2 = T

312 – 202 = U 49 + 85 = T 59 + 83 = D

249 – 72 = S 98 + 67 = E 369 ÷ 3 = I

34 x 4 = H

Answer:

....
134 136 165

....
225 110 256 177 123 142 125

37

Hide-and-seek

There are five starfish hiding among the fish and seaweed below. Find all five and write the coordinates of each one, noting down the letter first, then the number.

Answer: ....

Pattern prediction

Can you predict how many...

1. ...yellow squares will be in Pattern 4? ....

2. ...blue squares will be in Pattern 4? ....

3. ...yellow squares will be in Pattern 10? ....

4. ...blue squares will be in Pattern 50? ....

5. ...squares will make up Pattern 100? ....

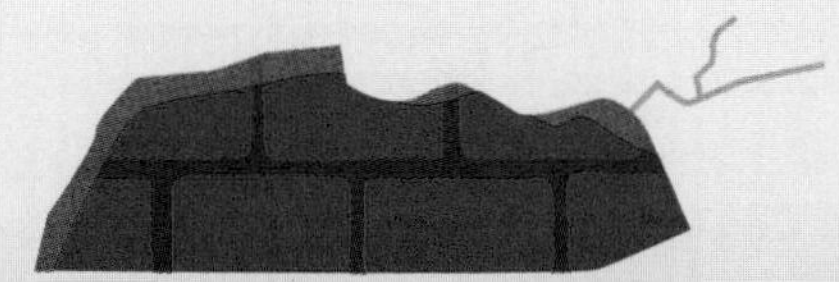

Folding shapes

The 2-D shapes on the left below can be folded to make the 3-D shapes on the right. Draw a line from each 2-D shape to the 3-D shape it can be folded into.

Two of a kind

Circle the two pictures that can be turned so that they match each other exactly.

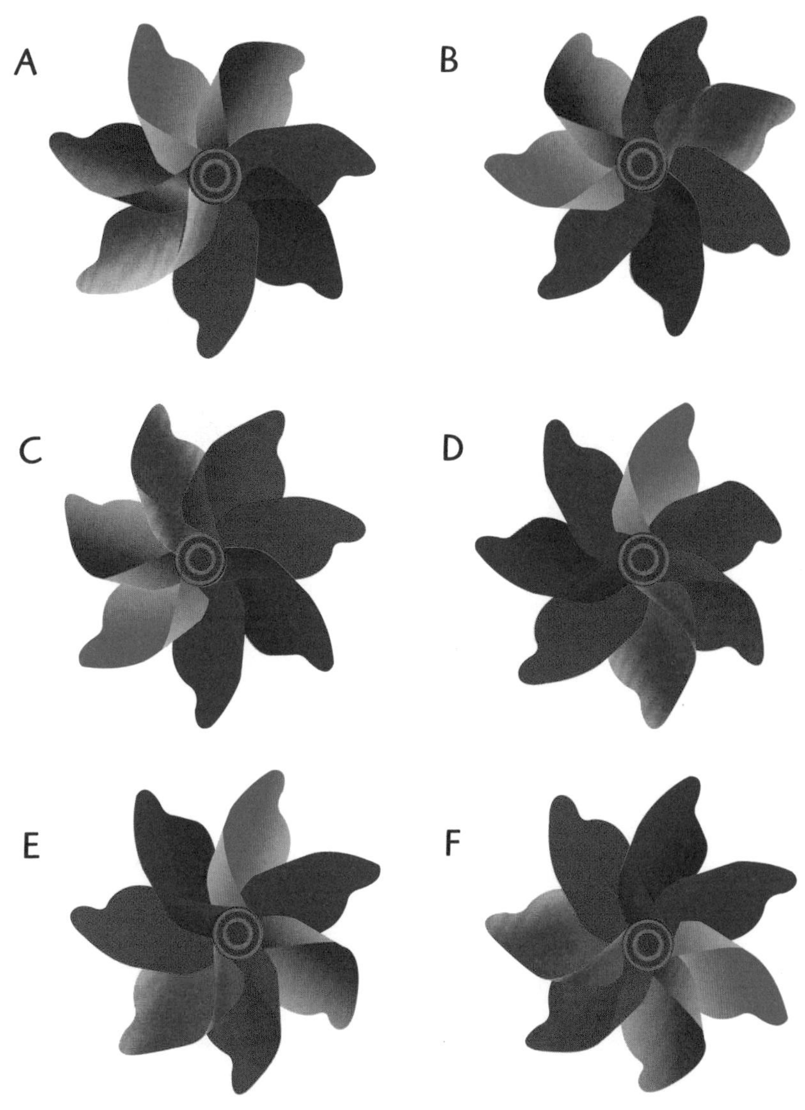

41

Christmas trees

The numbers in the round ornaments on each tree divide exactly into the number on its star. What numbers are missing from the trees? The first has been done for you.

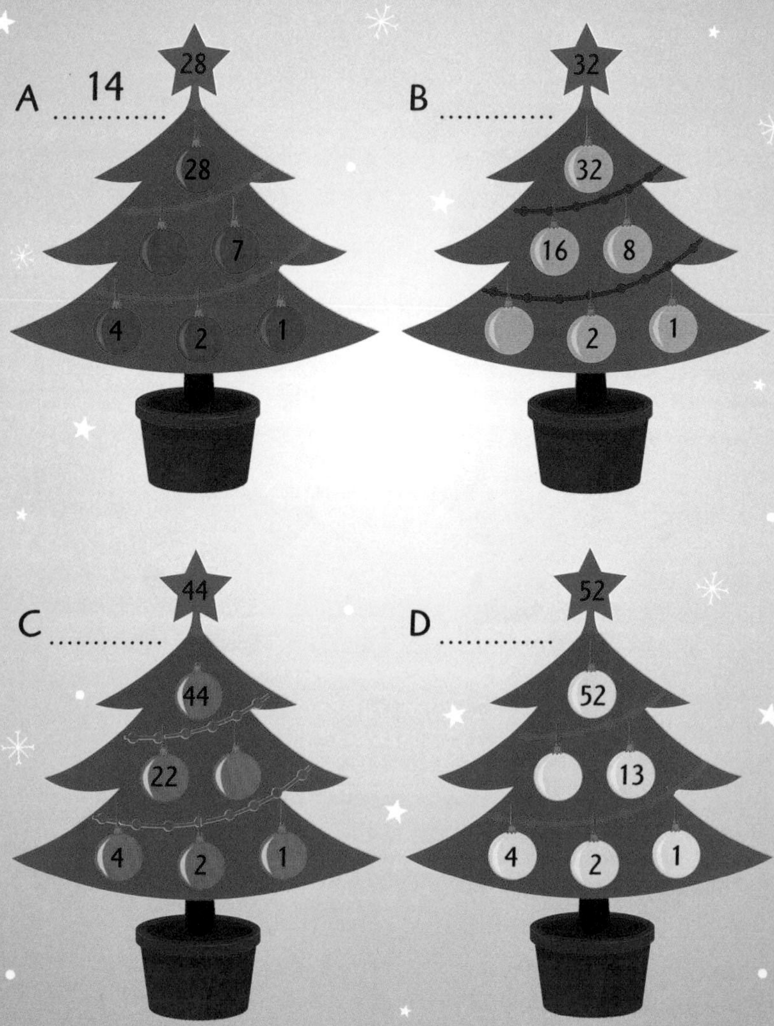

Moons and planets

The number on each planet is made by adding and subtracting the numbers on its moons in a particular order. Find the order, then write the correct number on the empty planet.

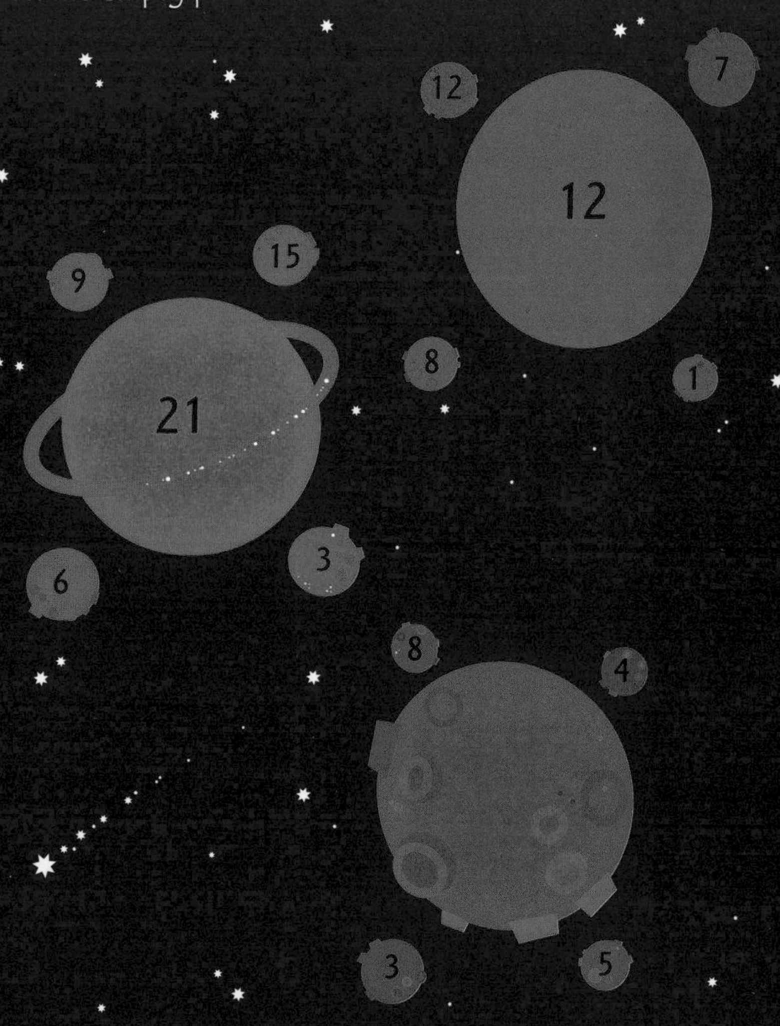

Jungle chart

Look closely at this scene, then finish the bar chart on the right.

Finish this bar chart, so that it shows the number of plants and animals in the scene on the left.

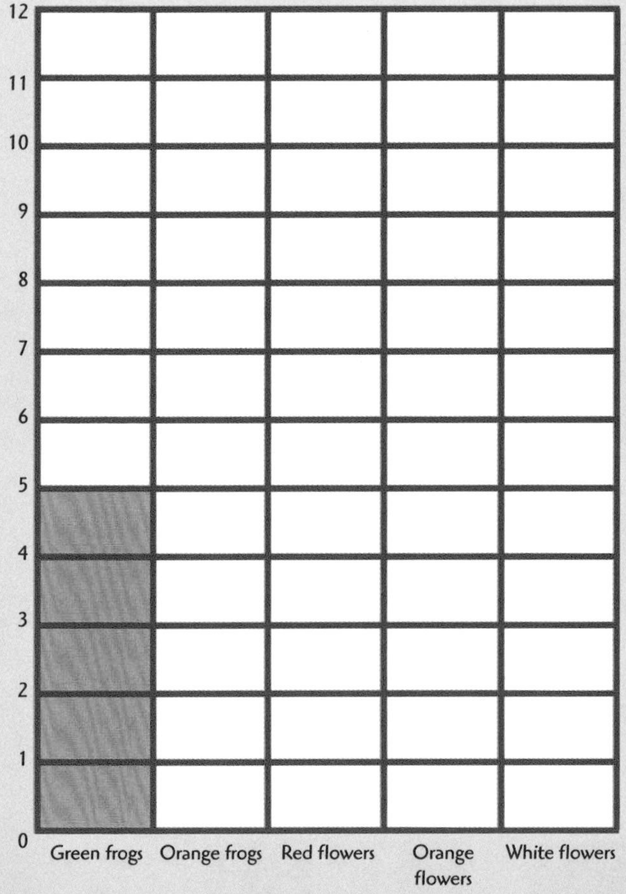

12
11
10
9
8
7
6
5
4
3
2
1
0

Green frogs | Orange frogs | Red flowers | Orange flowers | White flowers

Dominoes

Circle the domino that comes next in each sequence.

Sequence 1

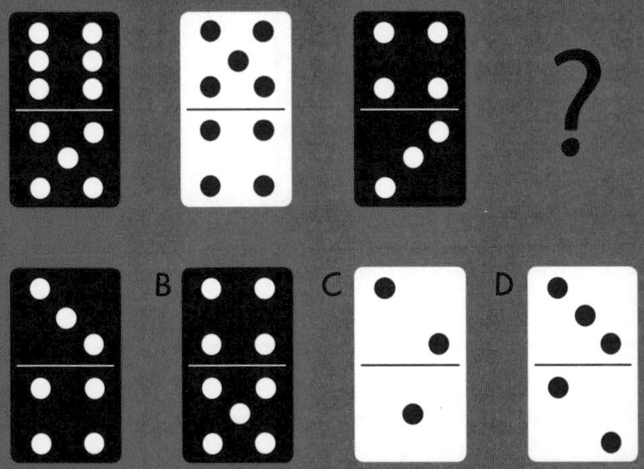

Sequence 2

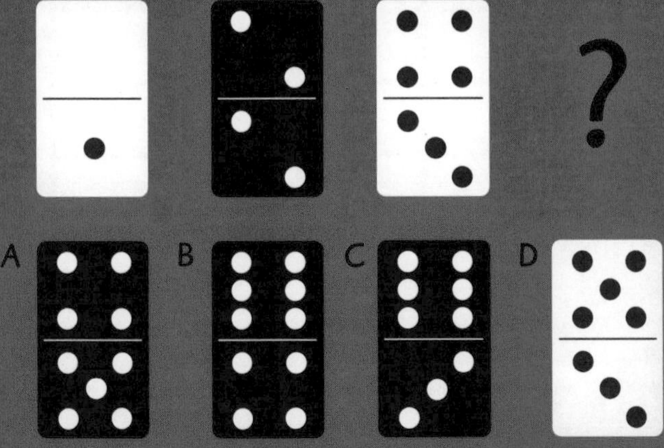

Cutting the cake

How can you cut a square cake into **eight** slices of equal size, with only **three** straight cuts? You can't move the slices as you cut. Draw three lines on the picture above to show where the knife would cut into the cake.

A rectangular cake is 6 units high × 11 units wide × 7 units deep. All its six sides are covered in pink frosting. If the cake is cut into 462 cubes measuring 1 × 1 × 1 unit, how many of these would have frosting on them?

Answer:...

Cross-sum

Fill in the blank squares with numbers from 1 to 9, so that the numbers in each row and column add up to the total shown in its arrow. (The direction of the arrows shows you whether to add across or down the grid.) You can only use a number once in an answer. For example, you can make 4 with 3 and 1, but not with 2 and 2.

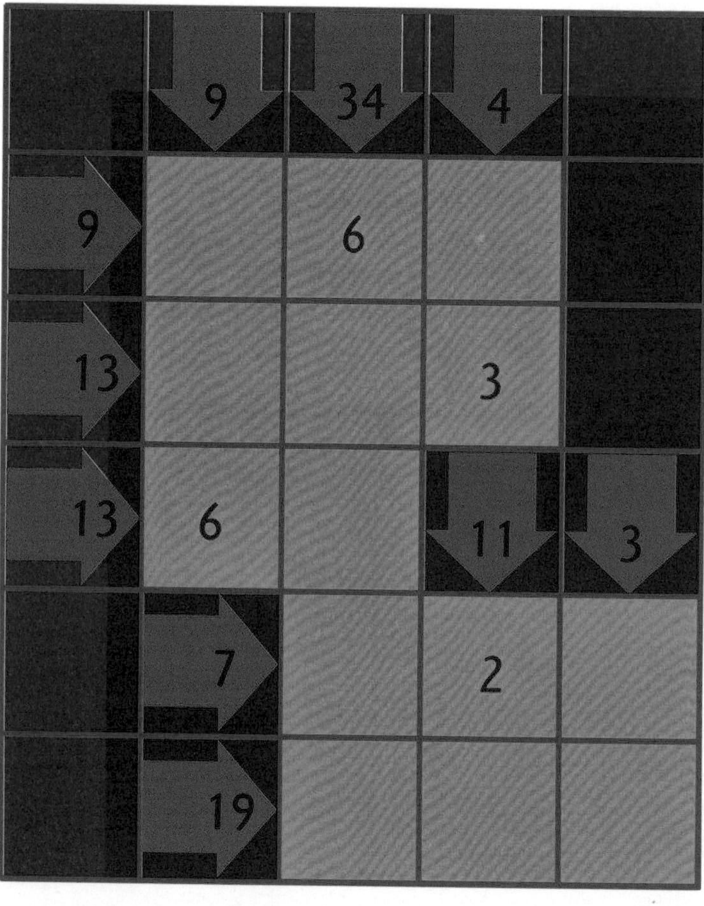

Furry friends

Sam takes her dog out for a walk three times a day. Over a period of two weeks, she spends 21 hours walking her dog. If all the walks are the same length of time, how long does each one last?

Answer:..

In a survey of 416 pet-owners, each one owned a dog or a cat or both. If there were 316 dog-owners and 280 cat-owners, how many of the dog-owners had no cats?

Answer:..

Amy and Jim work in an animal shelter and have to clean out the animals' cages every day. In a day, Amy can clean 13 cages, and Jim can clean ten. After a week, how many more cages would Amy have cleaned than Jim?

Answer:..

Calendar puzzle

OCTOBER						
Sun	Mon	Tue	Wed	Thu	Fri	Sat
		1	2	3	4	5
6	7	8	9	10	11	12
13	14	15	16	17	18	19
20	21	22	23	24	25	26
27	28	29	30	31		

What date is the day that is...

1. ... two days earlier than the day that is *four* days later than the day that is *one* week later than the day that is *five* days earlier than the day that follows Wednesday, October 23rd?

Answer:...

2. ... immediately following the day that is *two* days later than the day that is *four* days earlier than the day that is *one* week later than the day that is *two* days earlier than Tuesday, October 8th?

Answer:...

Life story

Ella the elephant spent the first $\frac{1}{4}$ of her life in the wild, then $\frac{1}{8}$ of her life in a circus. She spent $\frac{1}{2}$ of her life in a zoo. If Ella has spent the past nine years in an elephant sanctuary, how long did she spend in each place?

........years in the wild.

........years in the circus.

........years in the zoo.

Ella is .... years old.

Shape sequence

Draw the correct lines into the blank shape at the end of each of these sequences.

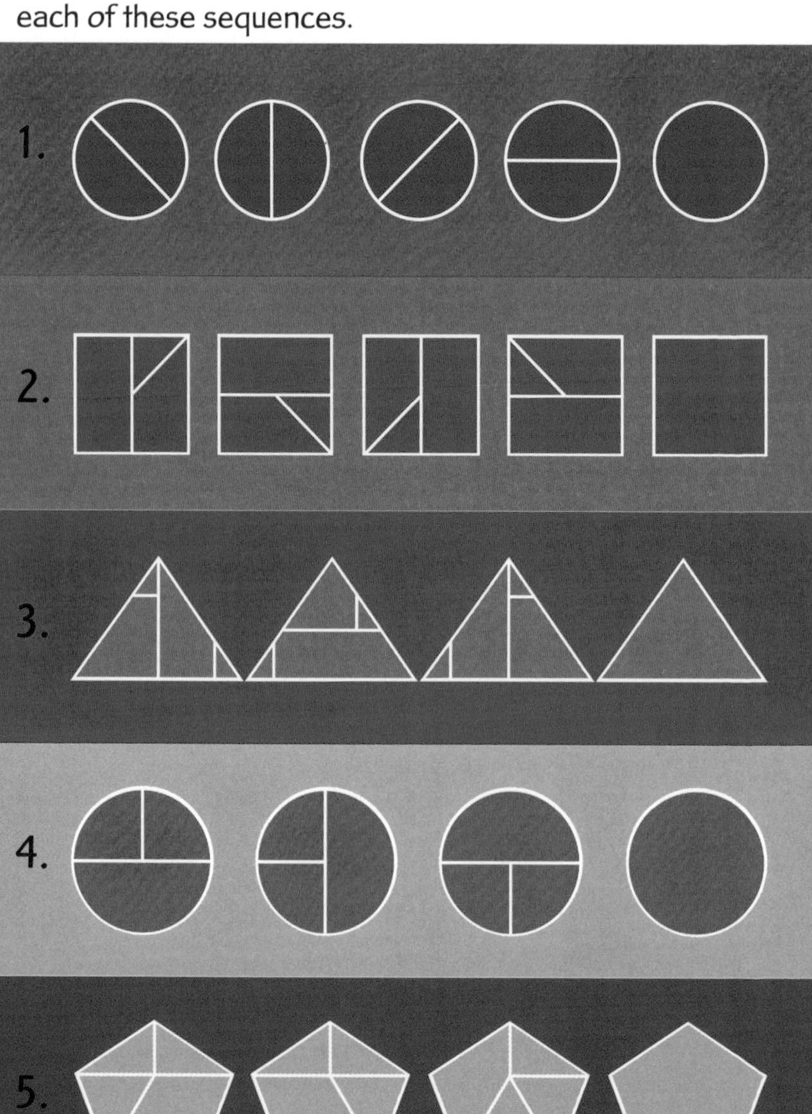

Missing angles

Calculate the missing angles in this picture. Use these rules to help you:

- Angles on a straight line add up to 180°.
- Angles inside a triangle add up to 180°.
- Angles inside a four-sided shape add up to 360°.

Answers:

a............... **b**............... **c**............... **d**...............

Picture code

The pictures in the grid below stand for the numbers 1, 2, 3 and 4, and the numbers around the edge are the sum of the numbers in each row or column. Can you work out which picture represents which number?

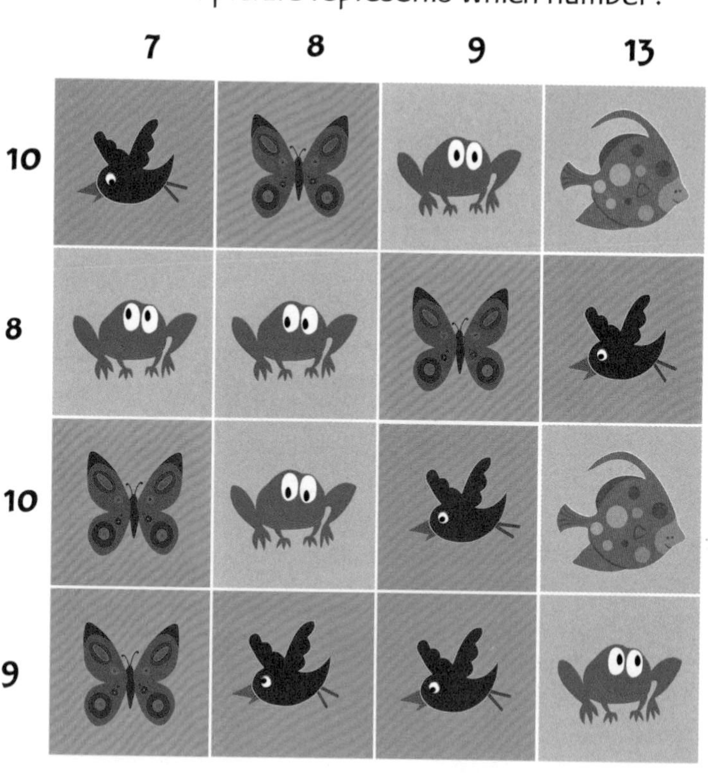

Answers:

Pick a card

Out of these cards, the chances of picking a queen are $\frac{2}{8}$, which is also $\frac{1}{4}$. What are the chances of picking...

1. ...a king? ....

2. ...a heart? ....

3. ...a red card? ....

4. ...the ace of spades? ....

5. ...the jack of diamonds? ....

Sudoku

This grid is made up of nine blocks, each containing nine squares. Fill in the blank squares, so that each block, row and column contains all the digits 1 to 9.

		7	8	5		1		
	3	1			2			6
		9	6		4			7
	7			9		6	5	
	5	2		6		9	8	
	9	4		3			1	
7			1		9	3		
9			3			2	7	
		8		2	6	4		

1 2 3 4 5 6 7 8 9

Dolphin training

The dolphins at Sandy Bay Sea Life Park are learning how to do tricks. Each one has its own trainer, who rewards it with a fish each time it does a trick. At the start of a training session, each trainer has ten fish.

- Blue does five tricks.
- Splash does two fewer tricks than Donny.
- Donny does one more trick than Blue.
- Dusky does three more tricks than Splash.

At the end of training, how many fish does each trainer have left?

Blue's trainer ....

Splash's trainer ....

Donny's trainer ....

Dusky's trainer ....

Function machine

A function machine changes numbers into other numbers. Fill in the blank buttons on the machine below to show what needs to happen to each number on the left to change it into the number on the right.

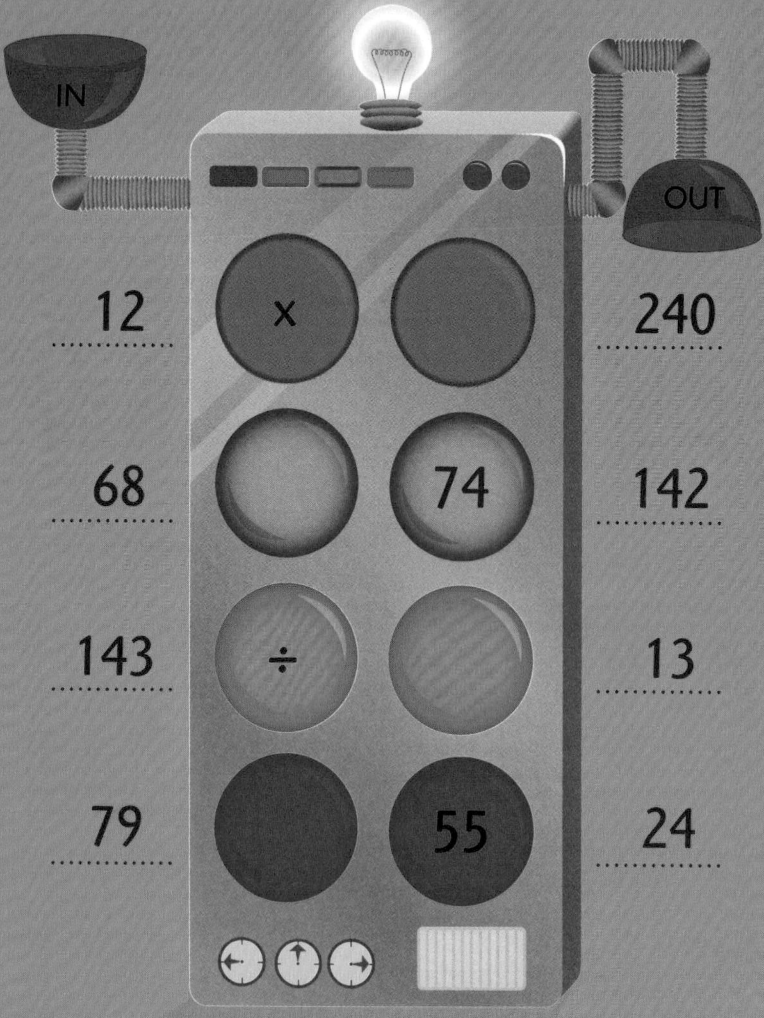

Pizza puzzle

Draw lines to connect the orders to the correct pizzas.

Table 1

$\frac{1}{2}$ mushroom

$\frac{1}{4}$ cheese

$\frac{1}{8}$ olives

$\frac{1}{8}$ pepperoni

A

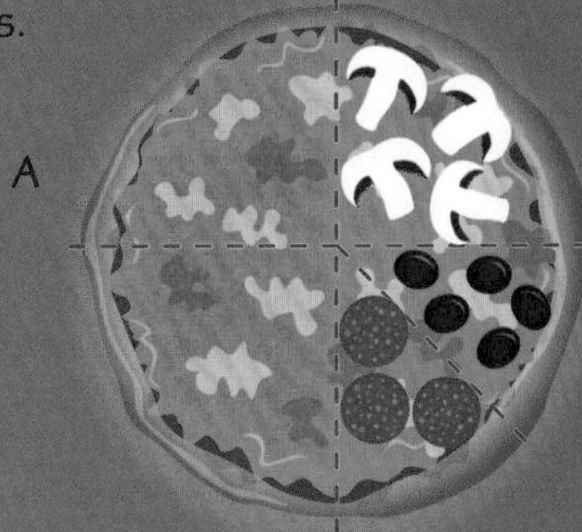

Table 2

$\frac{1}{2}$ cheese

$\frac{1}{4}$ mushroom

$\frac{1}{8}$ olives

$\frac{1}{8}$ pepperoni

B

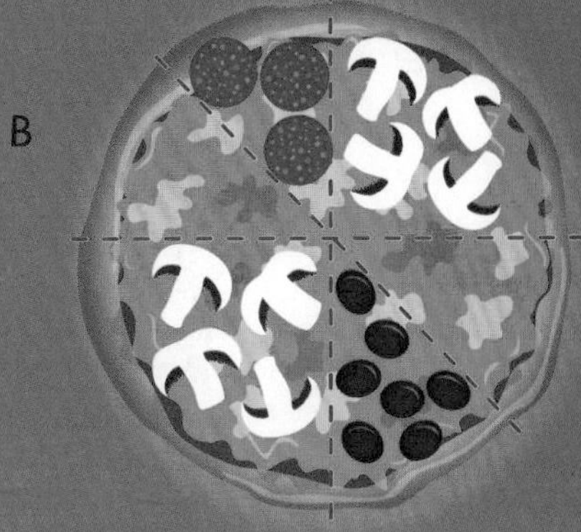

Table 3

$\frac{1}{2}$ cheese

$\frac{1}{4}$ olives

$\frac{1}{8}$ mushroom

$\frac{1}{8}$ pepperoni

C

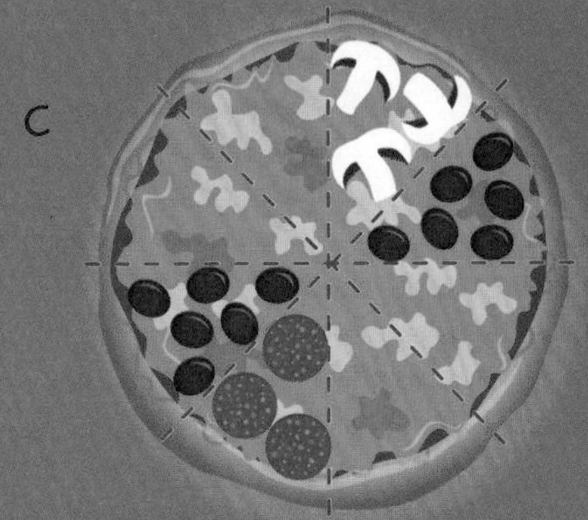

Fabulous footwear

Gigi the popstar has a large collection of shoes. One month, she buys 12 more pairs of shoes, but donates 36 pairs to charity. At the end of the month, she has 70 pairs of shoes. How many pairs did Gigi have at the beginning of the month?

Answer: ....

Dice pairs

Most of these pairs of dice have a total that matches that of another pair. Circle the pair that doesn't have a match.

Kite designs

Draw spots on 20% of the blank kite shapes below.
Then, draw squares on 25% of the kites left blank.
Next, draw stripes on $\frac{1}{3}$ of the kites that are blank.
Lastly, draw swirls on $\frac{1}{4}$ of the blank kites.

How many kites are left blank?

Answer: ....

Chore chart

Joe and Ellie are given stickers for doing household chores. Draw the stickers onto the chore chart below to find out who gets the most if:

Joe cleans his room twice, makes his bed twice, washes dishes once, and helps make dinner twice.
Ellie cleans her room once, makes her bed three times, washes dishes twice, and helps make dinner once.

CHORE CHART

- Cleaning room - 2 stickers
- Making your bed - 1 sticker
- Washing dishes - 1 sticker
- Helping with dinner - 2 stickers

Joe

Ellie

Answer: ....

Robot sequence

Look at the patterns on the screens of the robots in the top row. Then, circle the robot in the bottom row that should come next in the sequence.

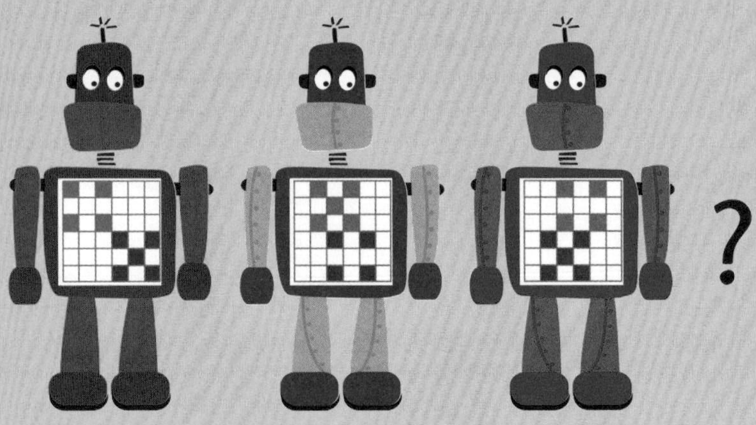

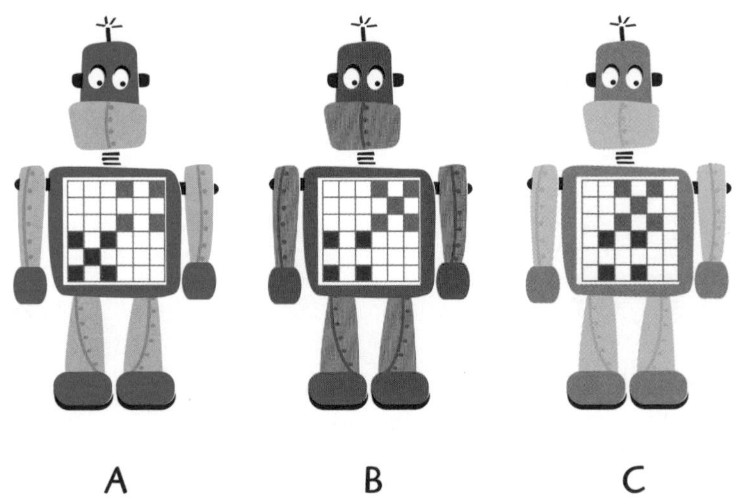

On the beach

There are 12 couples on the beach. One-third of the couples are there with two children, one-third are there with one child, and the last third have no children. How many people are on the beach?

Answer: ....

There are five times as many shells on the beach as there are children. How many shells are there?

Answer: ....

One quarter of the children build one sandcastle each, and one quarter of the children build two each. How many do they build altogether?

Answer: ....

Hopping along

A rabbit is hopping along the paths in a park. Look at the map of the park on the opposite page to calculate how many hops it would have to make to travel the shortest route...

...from the bench to the trees.

Answer:..

...from the trees to the bushes.

Answer:..

...from the trees to the swings, passing the pond.

Answer:...

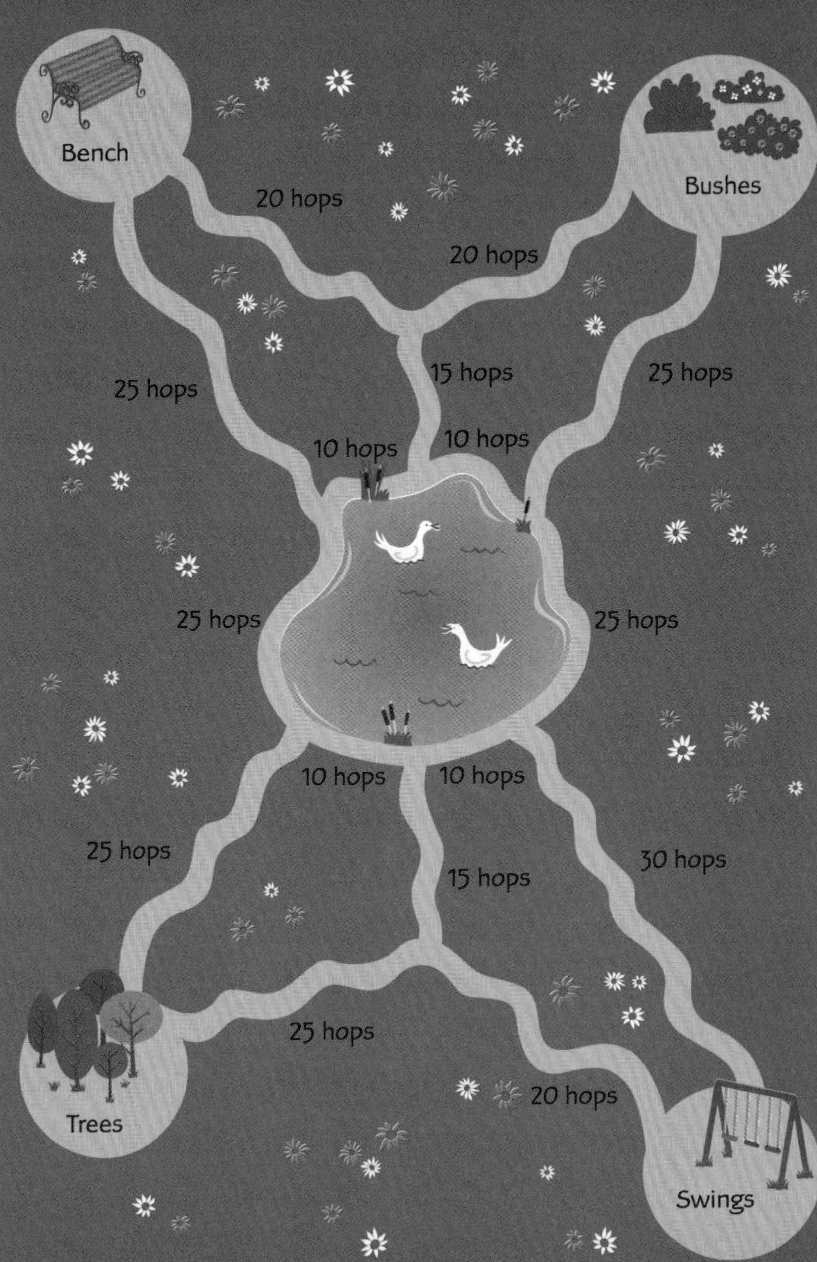

Bench
Bushes
20 hops
20 hops
15 hops
25 hops
25 hops
10 hops
10 hops
25 hops
25 hops
10 hops
10 hops
25 hops
15 hops
30 hops
25 hops
20 hops
Trees
Swings

Number search

See if you can find the answers to the questions below hidden in the grid. When you've found one, circle it, as shown on the right.

7	2	8	1	3	0	8	4
4	2	8	7	9	9	3	7
5	0	7	3	1	4	1	9
2	4	4	5	4	5	1	7
3	1	0	4	7	5	4	0
7	9	3	9	6	1	7	3
1	0	8	7	5	9	0	1
9	7	5	1	4	4	9	2

(25÷5)x7

(30x4)–6

(100–31)÷3

(8x6)+13

(64–52)x9

(7+5)x12

(70+18)÷4

(56÷7)+76

(99+9)÷9

At the movies

Surveys of a class of 15-year-olds were taken in 1980 and more recently, asking what kind of movies they liked the most. The results are shown in the pie charts below.

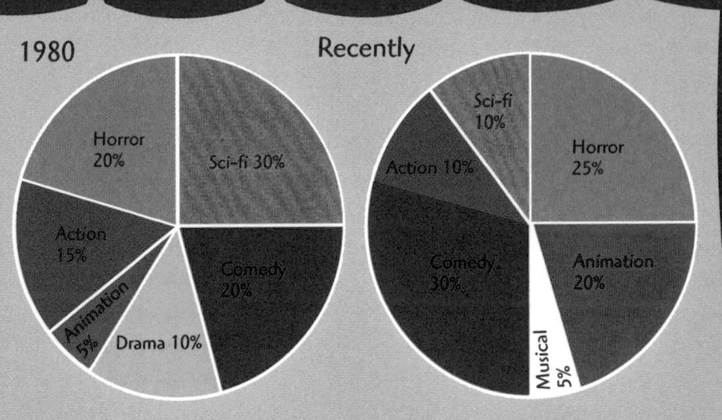

1. Which kind of movie has lost the most fans? ....

2. Which gained the most? ....

3. Which kind of movie is no longer popular? ....

4. Which kind is newly popular? ....

Picture subtraction

The pictures in the subtraction below have replaced the numbers 1, 2, 4 and 6. Which picture represents which number?

Answers:

 =

 =

 =

 =

Bubble burst

The bubbles below will burst if they contain a number that:

- is a multiple of nine
- is a square number
- is a prime number

Circle the bubble that won't burst.

Shape sorter

Draw lines to match the shapes to their descriptions.

A

- Four equal sides
- Opposite sides are parallel
- Opposite angles are equal

B

- Four sides
- One pair of parallel sides
- Parallel sides of different lengths

C

- Three sides
- No equal sides
- No equal angles

D

- Four sides
- Opposite sides are parallel
- No lines of symmetry

E

- Four sides
- No parallel sides
- One line of symmetry

Going to town

This pie chart shows how 24 people travel to town. How many people does each section represent? Use the angles to help you.

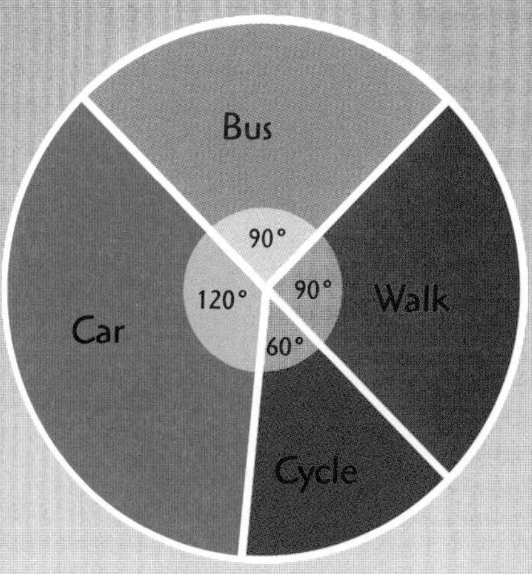

Number of people
Bus: ....
Car: ....
Cycle: ....
Walk: ....

Polar crossing

Help Pete the Polar Bear cross the water by drawing a line to mark his route. He can only step on ice-floe shapes that have a single line of symmetry.

After school

There are 30 children in a class. 20 of the children go to after-school clubs. Five go to drama club, four work on the school newspaper, eight play sports and three play in a band. Can you show this information in a pictogram? The first row has been done for you.

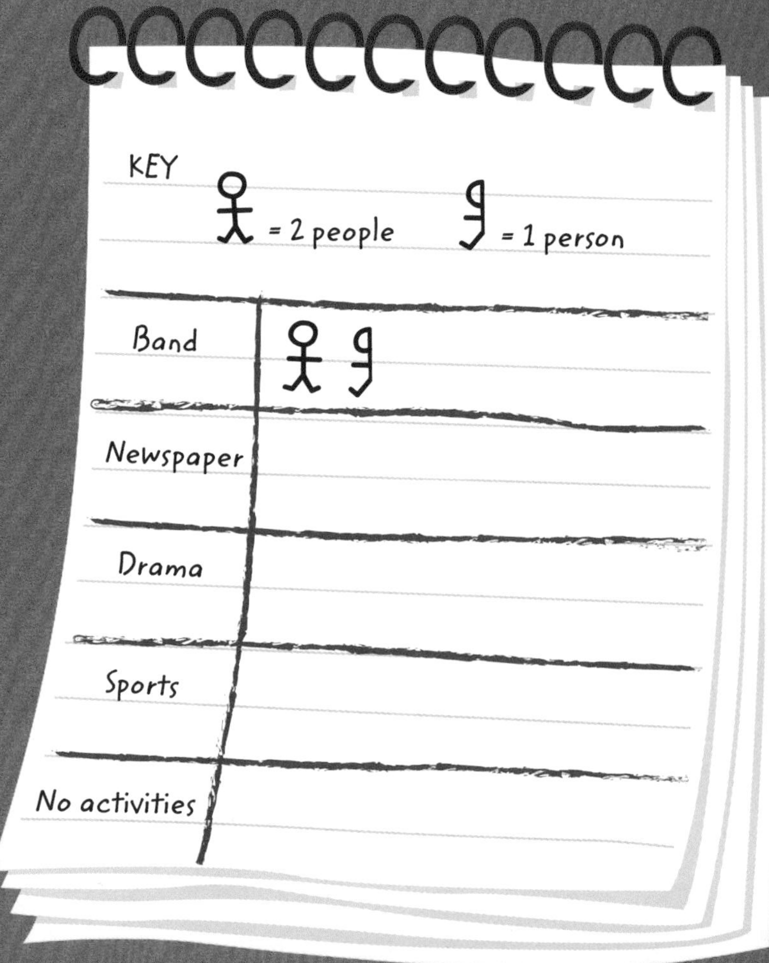

Sharing treasure

Pirate Jim is feeling generous. He decides to share the loot from his treasure chest with his crew.

- For every five rubies he takes for himself, he gives away one to his crew.
- For every 12 pearls he takes for himself, he gives four to his crew.
- For every 90 gold coins he takes for himself, he gives ten to his crew.

Pirate Jim takes 50 rubies, 240 pearls and 450 gold coins for himself. Before he shared them out, how many of each type of treasure was in the chest?

Rubies ....

Gold coins ....

Pearls ....

Seven silhouette

Shade in the shapes that contain numbers divisible by seven. What can you see?

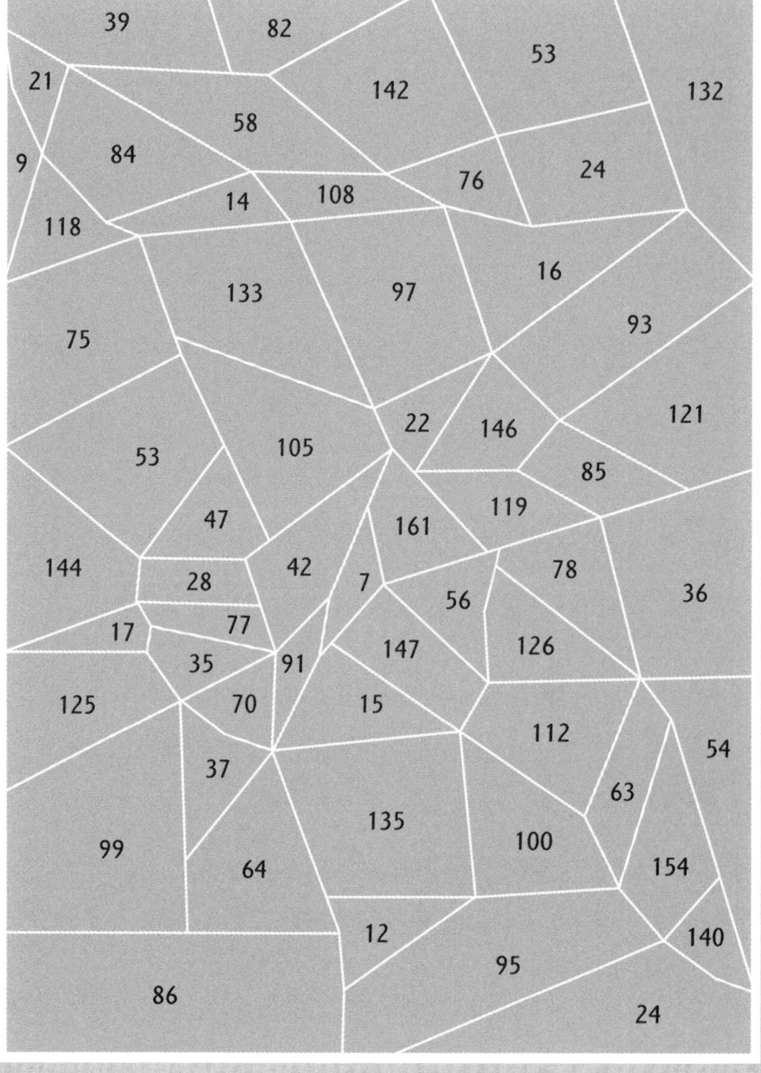

Whose room?

Here are plans of four bedrooms belonging to Bill, Ann, Tia and Sol. Use the clues below to discover which room is whose. Write the owner's name inside the plan of their room.

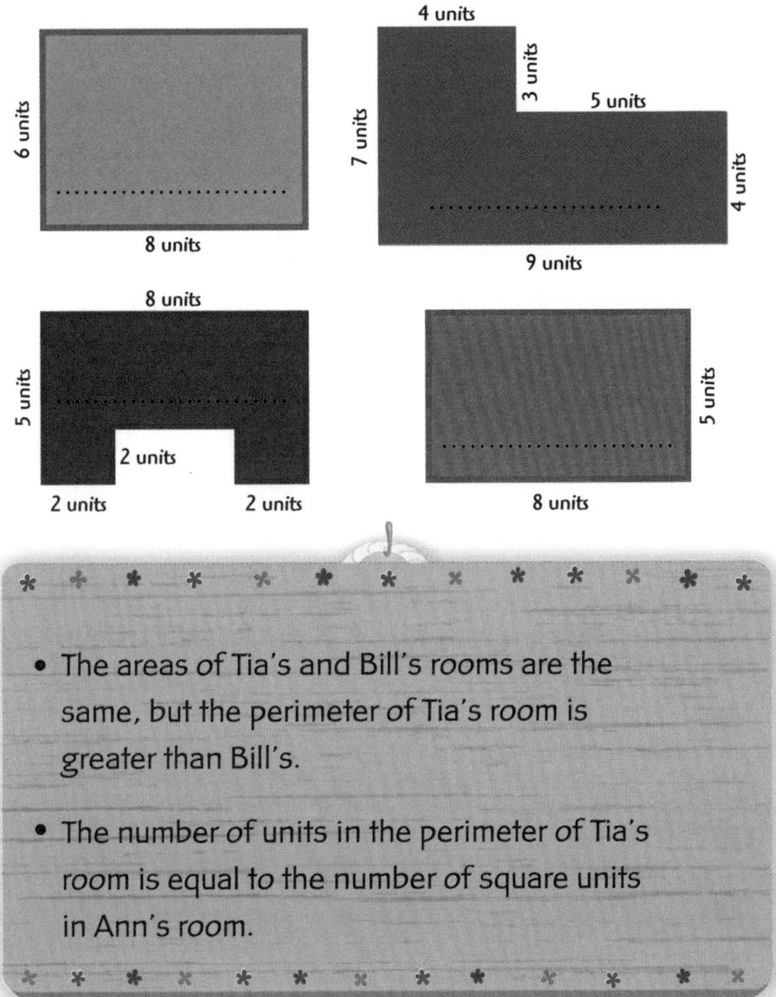

- The areas of Tia's and Bill's rooms are the same, but the perimeter of Tia's room is greater than Bill's.
- The number of units in the perimeter of Tia's room is equal to the number of square units in Ann's room.

Mouse maze

If the mouse takes the shortest route to the cheese, what is the sum of the numbers it passes through on the way?

Answer: ....

Reflections

On the grids below, the dotted blue lines are mirrors. Draw the reflection of each F-shape in the correct places on the grids.

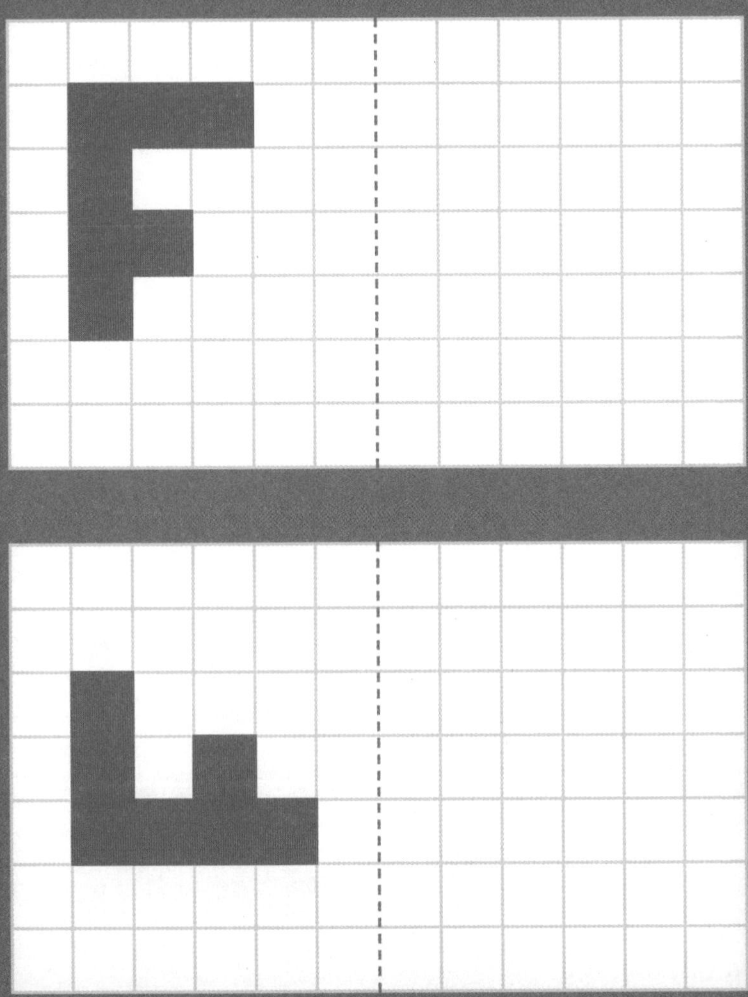

Buttons

Measure the distance from the middle of each button to the middles of all the other buttons. Which two pairs of buttons are exactly the same distance apart as each other?

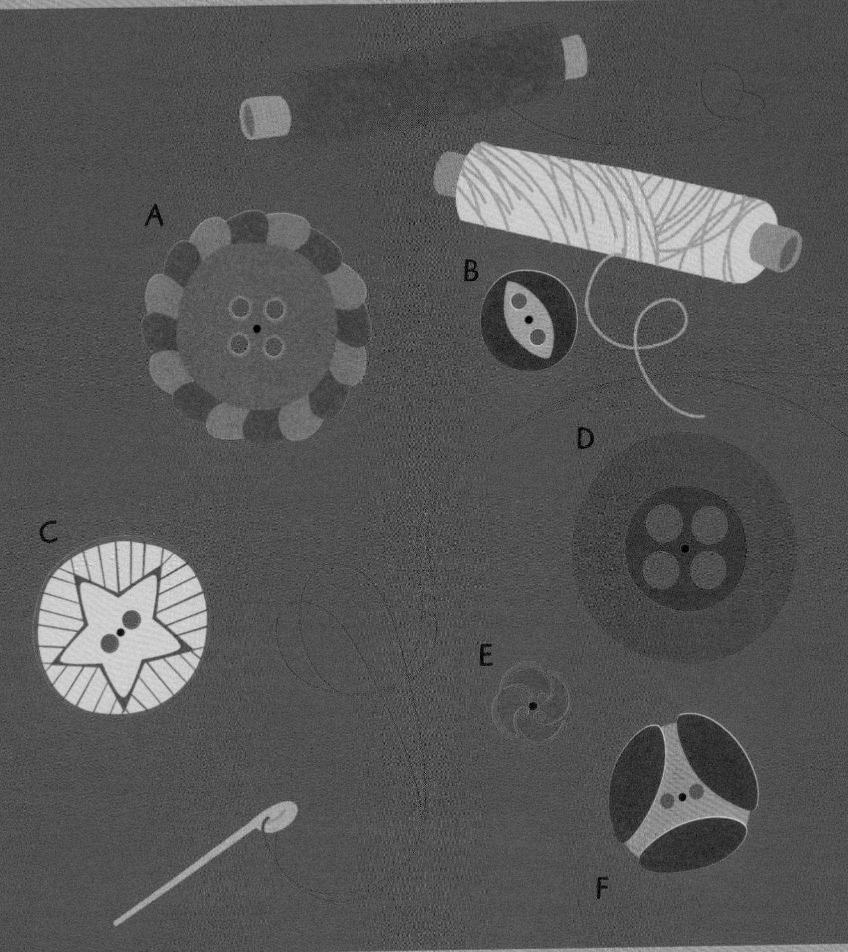

Answer: ....

Train times

Look at this train timetable, then answer the questions below it.

Departures

Barville	06:45	07:10	07:35	08:00	08:20	08:40
Clarkton	06:55	07:20	07:45	08:10	08:30	08:50
Mayfield	07:10	07:35	08:00	08:25	08:45	09:05
Everby	07:30	07:55	08:20	08:45	09:05	09:25

If you catch the 06:55 from Clarkton, then stop off in Mayfield for an hour and a half, when will be the next train from Mayfield to Everby?

Answer:...

How long is the journey from Barville to Everby?

Answer:...

If you have an appointment at 08:40 that is a ten-minute walk away from Mayfield station, what time is the latest train you can catch from Clarkton?

Answer:...

Breaking the code

Can you use this percentage code to read the hidden message?

CODE:

A	B	C	D	E	G	K	L
60% of 15	25% of 64	20% of 12	11% of 50	75% of 44	50% of 96	15% of 30	10% of 25

N	O	P	R	S	T	U	Y
30% of 70	80% of 10	40% of 90	1% of 80	70% of 35	5% of 60	21% of 20	2% of 45

MESSAGE:

0.9	8	4.2	9	0.8	33	9	48	0.8	33	9	3

2.4	8	5.5	33	16	0.8	33	9	4.5	33	0.8	

Pharaoh timeline

This timeline shows which pharaohs ruled Ancient Egypt between 1334BC and 1213BC.

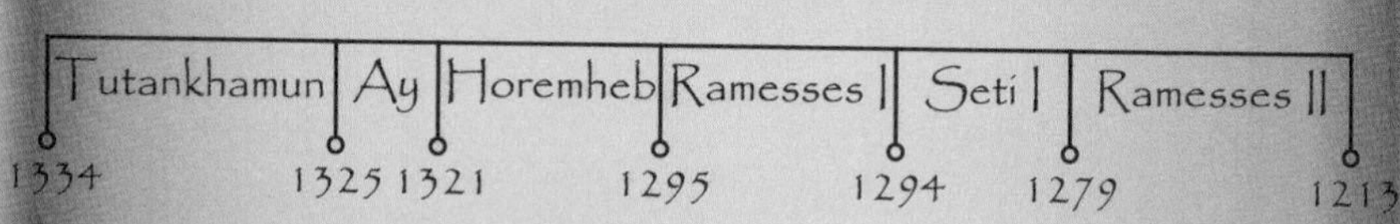

1. Circle the name of the pharaoh who had the shortest reign.

2. Underline the name of the pharaoh who had the longest reign

3. How long was Horemheb's reign? ....

4. If Tutankhamun came to the throne at age nine, how old was he when he died?

....

Balancing act

The scales below are evenly balanced. If you have 12 squares on one side, how many circles will you need to put on the other side for the scales to balance?

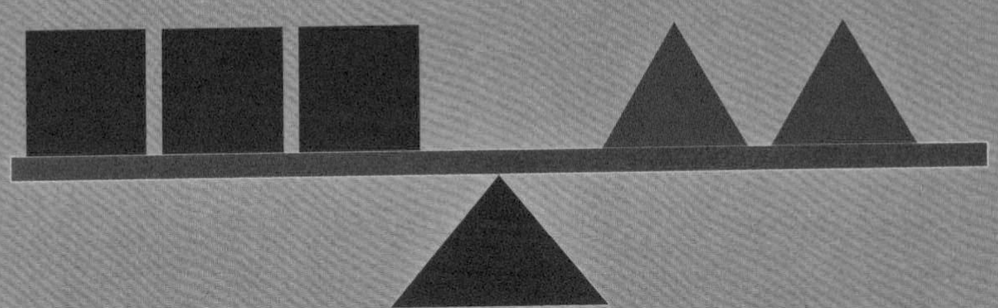

Answer: ....

Rainy days

Matt made a pictogram to show how many rainy days his town had during the first half of the year.

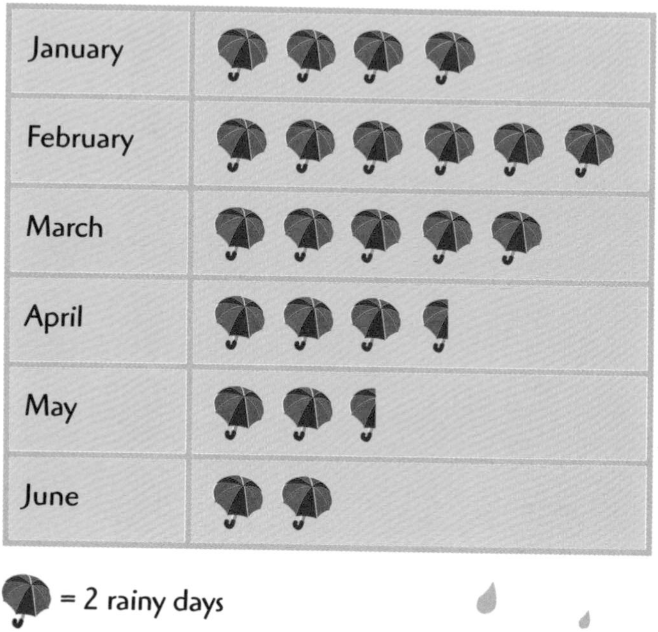

January	
February	
March	
April	
May	
June	

= 2 rainy days

True or false? Circle the correct letter.

1. There were six rainy days in May. T / F

2. March had one more rainy day than April. T / F

3. Only one month had over ten rainy days. T / F

4. There were 46 rainy days in total. T / F

Mirror image

Draw a mirror image on the right side of the grid to complete the picture.

Monster munchies

Three monsters are having a picnic. Halvilisk only eats pieces of food that are halves of the whole, Thirdathon eats thirds of the whole, and Sixthorax eats sixths. Look at the whole items of food below, then look at the pieces of food on the opposite page.

Draw lines to connect the pieces of pie, cake and chocolate to the monsters who will eat them.

Rag dolls

Granny Sue has started a new hobby: making rag dolls. This is the list of things she needs to make one doll:

1. How many buttons will Granny need to make one doll for each of her three granddaughters?

Answer:...

2. How many spools of thread will Granny need to make two dolls for each of her three granddaughters?

Answer:...

3. How many squares of fabric will Granny need to make three dolls for each of her three granddaughters?

Answer:...

Packing up

Finish filling in this table to show how many pallets, crates and boxes each type of fruit will fill, and how many pieces of fruit will be left unpacked.

Amount to be packed	Pallets (1,000 items each)	Crates (100 items each)	Boxes (10 items each)	Single items left unpacked
3,574 pineapples	3	5	7	4
30,922 bananas				
48,802 apples				
65,079 oranges				
101,430 strawberries				

Rounding

Round these numbers to the nearest 100:

1. 6,397 ....

2. 76,759 ....

3. 135,346 ....

4. 975,468 ....

5. 675,810 ....

6. 328,970 ....

Round these numbers to the nearest 1,000:

7. 57,390 ....

8. 901,357 ....

9. 1,543,851 ....

10. 6,931,576 ....

11. 8,308,622 ....

12. 9,159,975 ....

Cooking calculations

Janey is cooking for friends. The pie needs 50 minutes in the oven, and then it needs to stand for 15 minutes before serving. The potatoes need one hour in the oven to bake. The carrots take 15 minutes to cook and the peas need only three minutes. If Janey leaves herself five minutes to serve the food, can you draw lines to join the food to the time she needs to start cooking it, to have the meal on the table for 6:00 p.m.?

Cross-sum

Fill in the blank squares with numbers from 1 to 9, so that the numbers in each row and column add up to the total shown in its arrow. (The direction of the arrows shows you whether to add across or down the grid.) You can only use a number once in an answer. For example, you can make 4 with 3 and 1, but not with 2 and 2.

Missing symbols

Fill in the missing symbols to make each line true.
Use < for "is less than", > for "is more than" and = for "is equal to".

a. 0.03 .... 3%

b. ten million five hundred 1,000,500

c. 300,030 .... three hundred thousand and three

d. -100 .... -99

e. 60% .... $\frac{9}{15}$

f. eighty eight point eight 88.08

g. $\frac{11}{2}$ 5.5

h. $\frac{1}{3}$ 30%

i. 60.06 .... 60.6

j. $\frac{1}{8}$ .... $\frac{7}{49}$

Balancing act

A square, a triangle and a circle all weigh different amounts. The first two sets of scales below are evenly balanced, but the third set is not. Can you add the correct number of circles on the right-hand side to make it balance?

Number search

See if you can find the answers to the questions below hidden in the grid. When you've found one, circle it, as shown on the right.

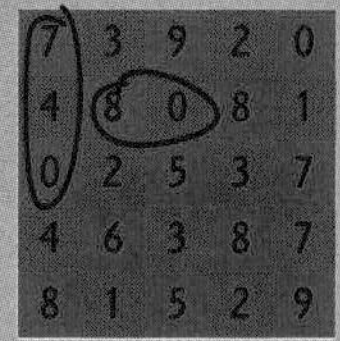

1	8	7	3	8	7	1	2
8	7	5	0	6	5	0	4
0	9	6	1	2	1	6	9
5	3	2	0	5	1	2	0
2	0	9	1	7	8	6	3
7	3	6	6	5	4	7	5
0	5	2	2	1	1	0	8
9	3	1	0	8	2	5	5

(44–37)x13

(32+64)÷4

(77x3)–152

(16+46)÷2

(59–48)x11

(42÷7)x14

(76÷4)+8

(88+77)÷3

(24x5)–82

Multiplying machine

Pick the correct odd and even number from the choices below to send through the machine to give the answer 104. Write one number on each dotted line.

19 23 21 8 10 6

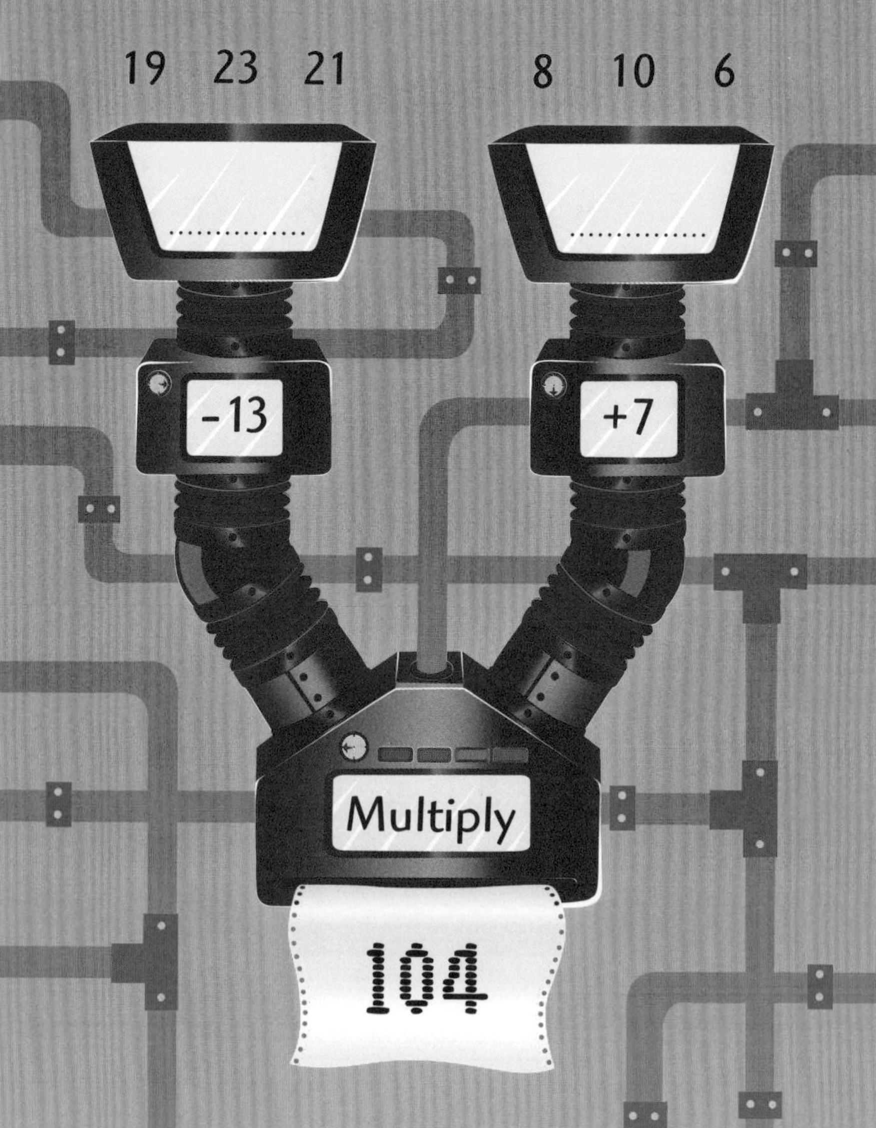

Dominoes

How many of these dominoes have a spots total that's...

...an odd number? ....

...a factor of 64? ....

...a prime number? ....

What percentage of the dominoes have a total number of spots that **isn't** any of the above? ....

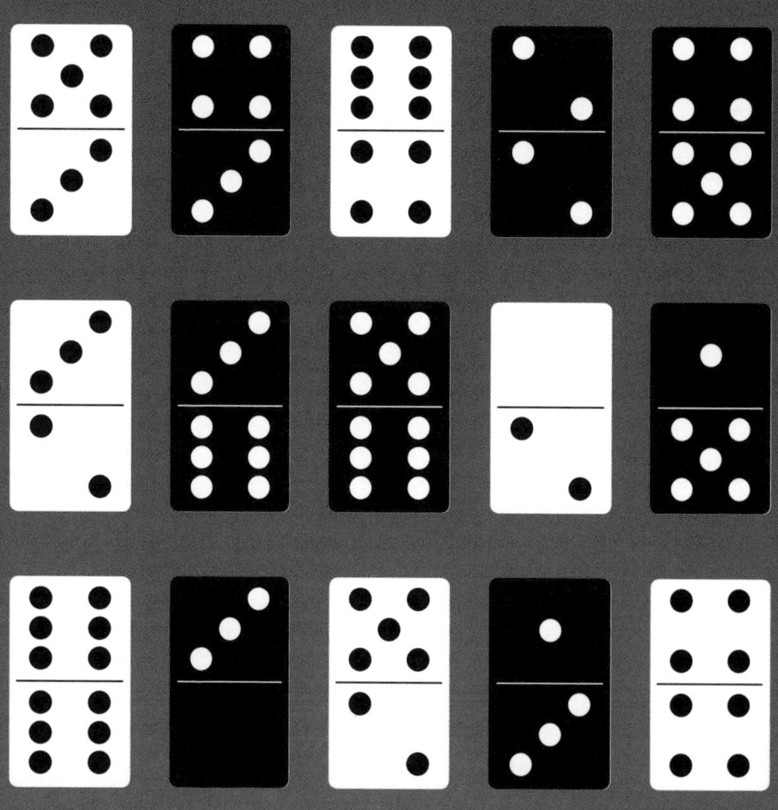

Sudoku

This grid is made up of nine blocks, each containing nine squares. Fill in the blank squares, so that each block, row and column contains all the digits 1 to 9.

	6		1		8			
		4		2		7		
3		8	7	4	5			
9		1					3	
	5	6	3	7	2	9	4	
	2					8		7
			2	5	6	3		4
7				1		6		
		2	4		7	1	9	

1 2 3 4 5 6 7 8 9

Cross-number

Use the clues to put the correct numbers into the grid.

Across →	Down ↓
2. 153,249 + 264,182	**1.** 3,001 – 1,156
4. eleven twentieths as a decimal.	**3.** fifteen million, twenty seven thousand and eighty
6. a quarter of 48,864	**5.** 80 x 70
9. 54,972,793 – 6,302,472	**7.** the number of legs on 5,070 elephants
10. eight million, eighty thousand and eight	**8.** the number of degrees in a right angle x 202

Rolling dice

When two identical six-sided dice are rolled together, there are 21 different possible outcomes (assuming that rolling 1 and 6 is the same as rolling 6 and 1). Writing your answers as fractions of 21, what is the probability of rolling...

...a two? ....

...a seven? ....

...an even number? ....

...a double? ....

...a multiple of three? ....

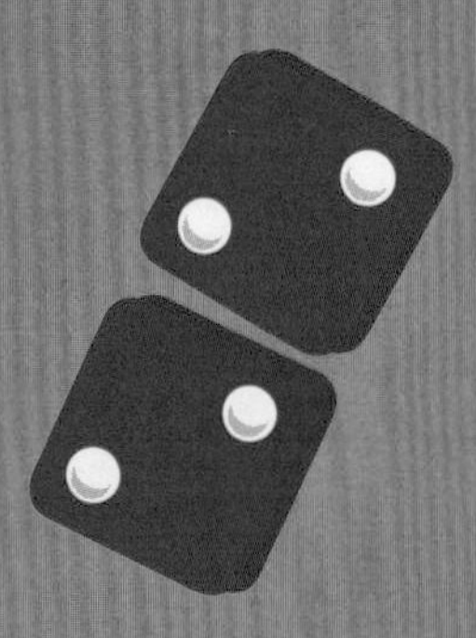

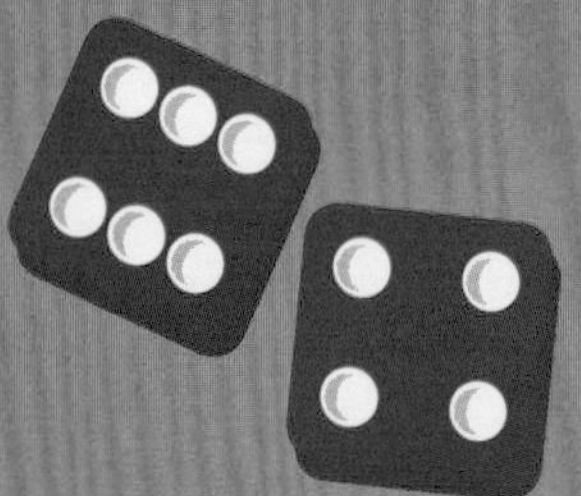

Tables test

Four friends each had a times tables test at school. Who scored the highest? Check the girls' answers, give them each a score and draw a star on the winning sheet.

Name Joanna

1x7=	7	6x7=	41
2x7=	14	7x7=	48
3x7=	21	8x7=	56
4x7=	28	9x7=	63
5x7=	35	10x7=	70

Score /10

Name Lizzie

1x8=	8	6x8=	48
2x8=	16	7x8=	56
3x8=	25	8x8=	62
4x8=	32	9x8=	74
5x8=	40	10x8=	80

Score /10

Name Alice

1x9=	9	6x9=	54
2x9=	18	7x9=	63
3x9=	26	8x9=	74
4x9=	37	9x9=	81
5x9=	45	10x9=	90

Score /10

Name Victoria

1x12=	12	6x12=	72
2x12=	24	7x12=	84
3x12=	36	8x12=	95
4x12=	48	9x12=	106
5x12=	62	10x12=	120

Score /10

Scribbling space

You can use the space on this page for any extra calculations you may want to do.

Answers

A

1. Town planning:

2. Train travel: 13

3. Space chart: a star

4. Dot-to-dot:

5. Toy sales: Dolls

6. Honeycomb:

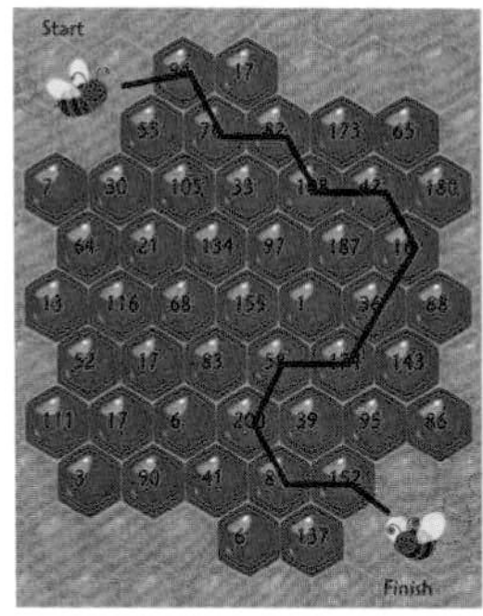

7. Milk monitor:
April – 7, Buttercup – 5, Clara – 6, Daisy – 2, Edna – 5

8. Bags and cases:
1. 3 2. 1 3. 2 4. 3 5. 1

9. Bubblegum machine:

red	Unlikely
yellow	Even chance
green *or* red	Impossible
blue	Likely
bubblegum	Definite

10. Long flight: 11:00 p.m., Tuesday, November 30th

11. Chocolate factory:
1. Milk chocolates
2. Chocolate caramels
3. 5,000

12. Towers and turrets:

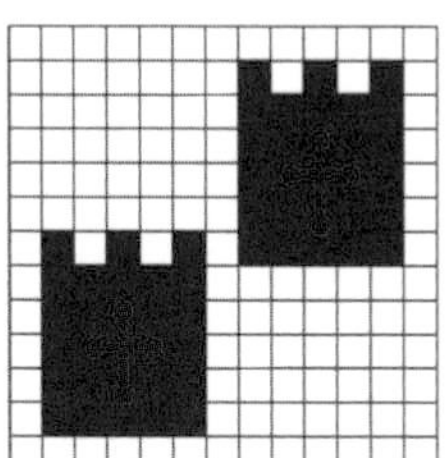

Answers

13. A game of golf:
1,200 steps

14. Missing symbols:
a.= b.< c.< d.> e.= f.>
g.< h.= i.= j.>

15. Pool party:

	Under 10	10-16	Total
American	5	3	8
British	7	4	11
German	9	9	18
French	6	4	10
Total	27	20	47

16. Market day: 3 coins

17. Gaming challenge:
1. 40 2. 4 3. 18

18. Parallel lines: C

19. Odd one out:
A. 52–48 B. 0.5x15
C. 60÷5 D. 0.2x220

20. Along the line:
1. 2.6 units 3. 2.4 units
2. 3.2 units 4. 5 units

21. Rabbit holes: 4

22. Counting cookies:
1. 24 2. 130

23. Triangle count: 37

24. Frogs and flies:
C, A, D, E, B

25. Crazy rides: 1. July
2. Crazy Coaster 3. 400

26. Cross-number:

		[1] 9		[2] 2	0	0	[3] 0	0	0
		9					.		
[4] 1	2	0	4	[5] 3	0	0	7		
0		9		6			5		
0				0					
[6] 0	.	2		3				[7] 8	
0				[8] 6	0	0	0	0	
1				0				8	
1								7	
	[9] 4	1	5	4	2	2	9	4	

27. Total Talent:
1. Mischa, Rob and Ellie
2. Jordan

Answers

28. On target:
40, 20, 10
50, 40, 10 or 50, 30, 20
50, 40, 30

29. Can tower:

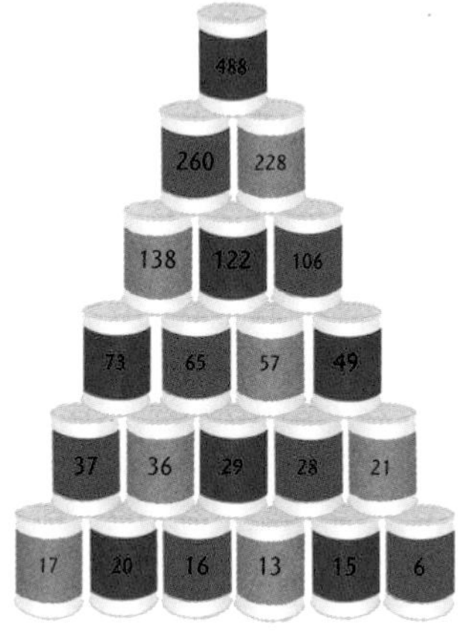

30. Safe cracker:
90, 10, 70, 30

31. Giant rocket:

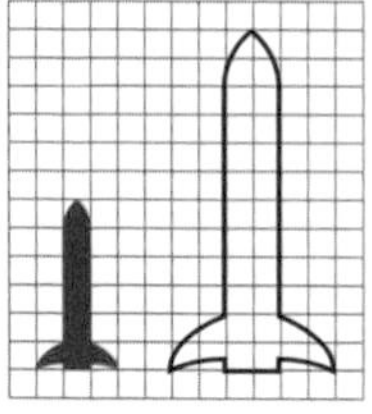

32. Inside numbers: 1. 4
2. 8 and 2 3. 1 and 9 4. 5

33. Gone fishing:

34. Gridlock:
20% red 25% black
50% silver

35. Bingo challenge: Ravi

36. Code calculator:
THE OUTSIDE

37. Hide-and-seek: (A,10)
(C,2) (D,11) (E,4) (G,8)

38. Pattern prediction: 1. 4
2. 5 3. 10 4. 51 5. 201

39. Folding shapes:

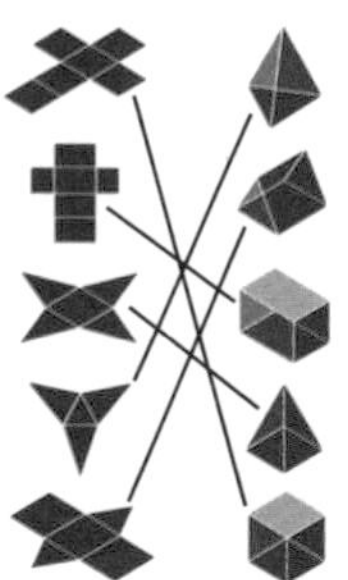

40. Two of a kind: B and F

Answers

41. Christmas trees:
A. 14 B. 4 C. 11 D. 26

42. Moons and planets:
8+4+5-3=14

43. Jungle chart:

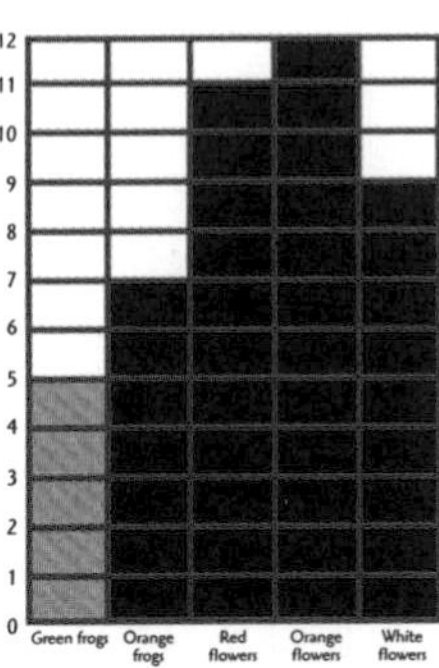

44. Dominoes: 1. D 2. B

45. Cutting the cake:
Make two straight or two diagonal cuts through the top of the cake, cutting it into half, then into quarters. Then, make a third, horizontal cut through the middle of the whole cake. 282 – the core of the cake would be 4 × 9 × 5 units, containing 180 cubes. Out of 462 cubes, the remaining 282 cubes would have one, two or three sides with frosting.

46. Cross-sum:

47. Furry friends:
30 minutes 136 21 cages

48. Calendar puzzle:
1. October 28th
2. October 12th

49. Life story:
18 years in the wild. 9 years in the circus. 36 years in the zoo. Ella is 72 years old.

50. Shape sequence:

51. Missing angles:
a=45° b=60° c=55° d=120°

52. Picture code:
= 1 = 2 = 3 = 4

Answers

53. Pick a card: 1. $\frac{1}{4}$
2. $\frac{3}{8}$ 3. $\frac{1}{2}$ 4. $\frac{1}{8}$ 5. *0*

54. Sudoku:

4	6	7	8	5	3	1	2	9
5	3	1	9	7	2	8	4	6
2	8	9	6	1	4	5	3	7
8	7	3	2	9	1	6	5	4
1	5	2	4	6	7	9	8	3
6	9	4	5	3	8	7	1	2
7	2	5	1	4	9	3	6	8
9	4	6	3	8	5	2	7	1
3	1	8	7	2	6	4	9	5

55. Dolphin training:
Blue's trainer 5
Splash's trainer 6
Donny's trainer 4
Dusky's trainer 3

56. Function machine:

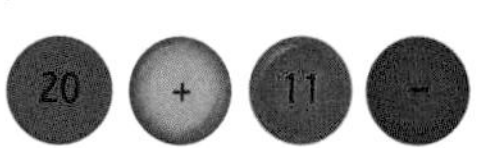

57. Pizza puzzle:
1. B 2. A 3. C

58. Fabulous footwear: 94

59. Dice pairs:

60. Kite designs: 3

61. Chore chart: *Joe*

62. Robot sequence: B

63. On the beach:
36 people 60 shells
9 sandcastles

64. Hopping along:
75 95 70

65. Number search:

7	2	8	1	3	0	8	4
4	2	8	7	9	9	3	7
5	0	7	3	1	4	1	9
2	4	4	5	4	5	1	7
3	1	0	4	7	5	4	0
7	9	3	9	6	1	7	3
1	0	8	7	5	9	0	1
9	7	5	1	4	4	9	2

66. At the movies:
1. Sci-fi 2. Animation
3. Drama 4. Musical

67. Picture subtraction:

68. Bubble burst: 26

Answers

69. Shape sorter:

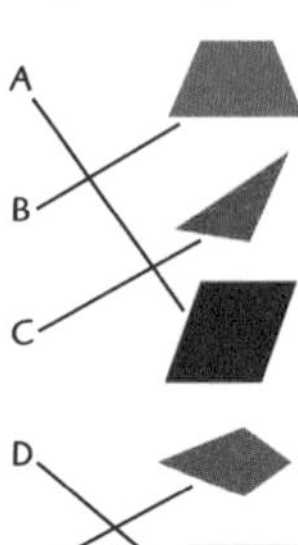

70. Going to town:
Bus: 6 Cycle: 4
Car: 8 Walk: 6

71. Polar crossing:

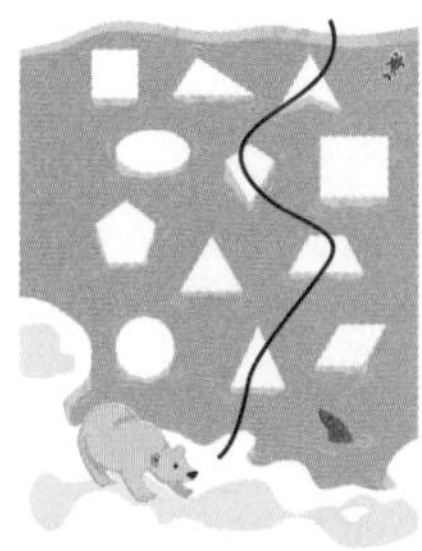

72. After school:

Band	
Newspaper	
Drama	
Sports	
No activities	

73. Sharing treasure:
Rubies - 60 Pearls - 320
Gold coins - 500

74. Seven silhouette:

75. Whose room?:

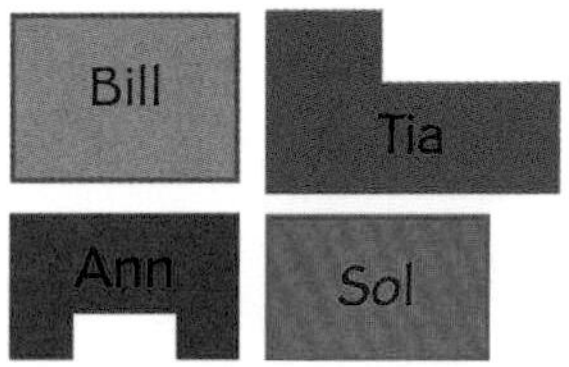

76. Mouse maze: 68

77. Reflections:

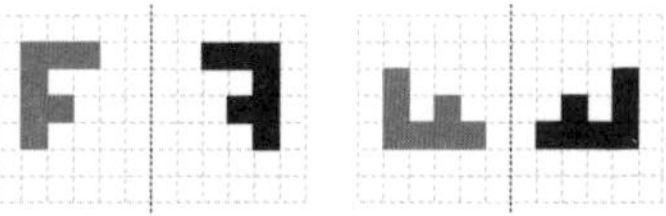

78. Buttons: A and B, B and D

79. Train times: 08:45
45 minutes 08:10

Answers

80. Breaking the code:
YOU ARE A GREAT CODE BREAKER

81. Pharaoh timeline:
1. Ramesses I 2. Ramesses II
3. 26 years 4. 18

82. Balancing act: 6

83. Rainy days:
1. F 2. F 3. T 4. T

84. Mirror image:

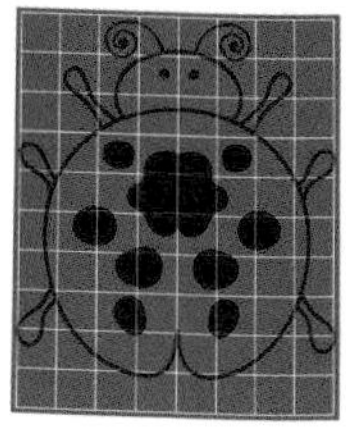

85. Monster munchies:

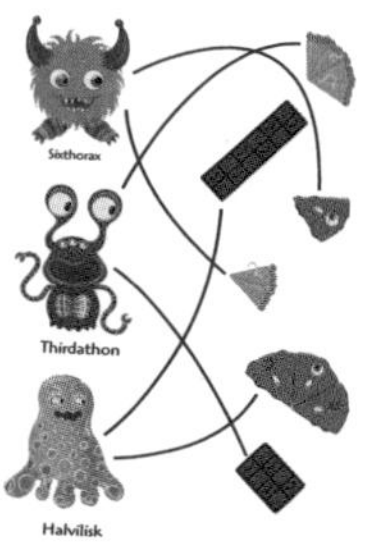

86. Rag dolls: 1. 6 2. 12 3. 45

87. Packing up:

3,574 pineapples	3	5	7	4
30,922 bananas	30	9	2	2
48,802 apples	48	8	0	2
65,079 oranges	65	0	7	9
101,430 strawberries	101	4	3	0

88. Rounding:

1. 6,400 4. 975,500
2. 76,800 5. 675,800
3. 135,300 6. 329,000

7. 57,000 10. 6,932,000
8. 901,000 11. 8,309,000
9. 1,544,000 12. 9,160,000

89. Cooking calculations:

Answers

90. Cross-sum:

91. Missing symbols:

a. = b. > c. > d. < e. =

f. > g. = h. > i. < j. <

92. Balancing act:

Two circles

93. Number search:

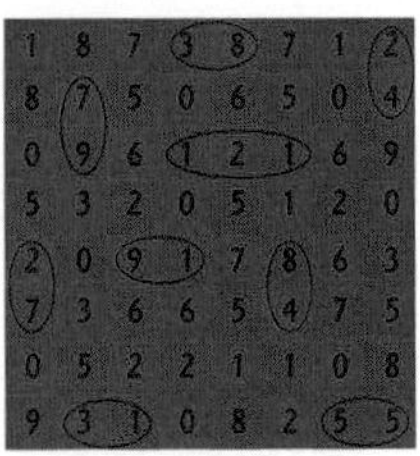

94. Multiplying machine:

21 and 6

95. Dominoes:

7, 5, 6, 20%

96. Sudoku:

2	6	7	1	3	8	4	5	9
5	1	4	6	2	9	7	8	3
3	9	8	7	4	5	2	1	6
9	7	1	8	6	4	5	3	2
8	5	6	3	7	2	9	4	1
4	2	3	5	9	1	8	6	7
1	8	9	2	5	6	3	7	4
7	4	5	9	1	3	6	2	8
6	3	2	4	8	7	1	9	5

97. Cross-number:

98. Rolling dice:

$\frac{1}{21}$ $\frac{3}{21}$ $\frac{12}{21}$ $\frac{6}{21}$ $\frac{7}{21}$

99. Tables test:

Joanna: *8 out of 10*

Lizzie: *7 out of 10*

Alice: *7 out of 10*

Victoria: *7 out of 10*

First published in 2015 by Usborne Publishing Ltd, 83-85 Saffron Hill, London EC1N 8RT, England.

First published in America in 2016. AE.